DEVELOPING
GROWTH
MINDSETS

Other Books by Donna Wilson and Marcus Conyers

Teaching Students to Drive Their Brains:
Metacognitive Strategies, Activities, and Lesson Ideas

ASCD MEMBER BOOK

Many ASCD members received this book as a
member benefit upon its initial release.

Learn more at: **www.ascd.org/memberbooks**

DONNA **WILSON**   MARCUS **CONYERS**

DEVELOPING
GROWTH
MINDSETS

Principles and Practices
for Maximizing Students' Potential

Alexandria, Virginia USA

1703 N. Beauregard St. • Alexandria, VA 22311-1714 USA
Phone: 800-933-2723 or 703-578-9600 • Fax: 703-575-5400
Website: www.ascd.org • E-mail: member@ascd.org
Author guidelines: www.ascd.org/write

Ranjit Sidhu, *CEO & Executive Director*; Stefani Roth, *Publisher*; Genny Ostertag, *Director, Content Acquisitions*; Julie Houtz, *Director, Book Editing & Production*; Joy Scott Ressler, *Editor*; Judi Connelly, *Senior Art Director*; Thomas Lytle, *Associate Art Director*; Valerie Younkin, *Production Designer*; Kelly Marshall, *Manager, Production Services*; Shajuan Martin, *E-Publishing Specialist*.

PAPERBACK ISBN: 978-1-4166-2914-6   ASCD product #120033

PDF E-BOOK ISBN: 978-1-4166-2916-0; see Books in Print for other formats.

Quantity discounts are available: e-mail programteam@ascd.org or call 800-933-2723, ext. 5773, or 703-575-5773. For desk copies, go to www.ascd.org/deskcopy.

ASCD Member Book No. FY20-7 (May 2020 P). ASCD Member Books mail to Premium (P), Select (S), and Institutional Plus (I+) members on this schedule: Jan, PSI+; Feb, P; Apr, PSI+; May, P; Jul, PSI+; Aug, P; Sep, PSI+; Nov, PSI+; Dec, P. For current details on membership, see www.ascd.org/membership.

Library of Congress Cataloging-in-Publication Data
Names: Wilson, Donna (Psychologist), author. | Conyers, Marcus, author.
Title: Developing growth mindsets: principles and practices for maximizing students' potential / by Donna Wilson and Marcus Conyers.
Description: Alexandria, Virginia: ASCD, [2020] | Includes bibliographical references and index.
Identifiers: LCCN 2019051646 (print) | LCCN 2019051647 (ebook) | ISBN 9781416629146 (paperback) | ISBN 9781416629160 (pdf)
Subjects: LCSH: Learning, Psychology of. | Learning—Physiological aspects. | Achievement motivation.
Classification: LCC LB1060.W5526 2020 (print) | LCC LB1060 (ebook) | DDC 370.15/23—dc23
LC record available at https://lccn.loc.gov/2019051646
LC ebook record available at https://lccn.loc.gov/2019051647

28 27 26 25 24 23 22 21 20   1 2 3 4 5 6 7 8 9 10 11 12

We dedicate this book to educators we work with around the world who are empowering their students with the growth mindsets, skills, and knowledge they need to flourish and maximize their unique potential.

DEVELOPING
GROWTH
MINDSETS

Acknowledgments

— —

We are continually inspired by the many educators who earned their graduate degrees with us focused on applied mind, brain, and education science (BrainSMART programs) with Nova Southeastern University or attended our professional development workshops. And we appreciate that they have shared with us the positive results they are achieving in their classrooms and schools. Within the pages of this book, you will find stories and perspectives from our graduates that exemplify the power of growth mindsets; these educators applied the knowledge, skills, and teaching and learning methods presented here in their professional practices. We thank Cecilia Beagle, Leanne Caparro, Diane Dahl, Michael Fitzgerald, D'Jon McNair, Kelly Rose, Maureen Ryan, and Melissa Smith for sharing their stories.

We appreciate the contributions from our editors Karen Bankston and Diane Franklin. In addition to their assistance in editing our work, we want to express our gratitude for their work in interviewing some of the teachers whose stories are shared here. Thanks also to Lorraine Ortner-Blake for creating the graphics that illustrate key concepts in this book. A big thank you to our wonderful team at ASCD, including the amazing Genny Ostertag,

Joy Scott Ressler, Stefani Roth, and Thomas Lytle. We appreciate the many communications that we had with project manager Joy Scott, and the care that the publishing team took in presenting our work.

Finally, we acknowledge the significance of our own love, partnership, and life together in growing our mindsets and thriving in the work we do and enjoy.

Introduction

- -

The developmental sculpting of the brain's networks through
learning is akin to the process of growing a botanical garden.
—Mary Helen Immordino-Yang,
Linda Darling-Hammond, and Christina Krone,
The Brain Basis for Integrated Social, Emotional,
and Academic Development (2018, p. 1)

Every school day, learners of all ages arrive in classrooms, each with a brain powered by some 86 billion neurons. Many of these neurons make approximately 10,000 connections to other neurons, which is an astounding amount of activity. Just one cubic centimeter of the human brain is estimated to have as many connections as there are stars in the Milky Way galaxy. Breakthrough research indicates that learning changes the structure and function of the brain and that the creation, strengthening, and pruning of neural connections are key to the learning process.

In essence, human beings have tremendous potential to acquire new knowledge, develop new skills, and improve their brains throughout life. Applying effective learning strategies enhances this process. These vital discoveries from mind, brain, and education research are seldomly explicitly taught to students, and this information is not necessarily a major emphasis in teacher education programs. We stand at a unique time in human history, with the opportunity to empower all learners through an understanding of their brains' awesome capacity to change as the result of learning and to equip them with practical learning strategies that can significantly improve the growth of knowledge and skills.

In our work with teachers, we have found that explicitly teaching fundamentals of brain plasticity is a critical component for fostering what Stanford University psychologist Carol Dweck describes as a *growth mindset* (2016a, 2019). Discovering that learning changes their brains helps students develop this mindset—the belief that they can improve their knowledge and skills through the use of learning strategies and with guidance and support from teachers, coaches, and mentors. In a very real sense, understanding brain plasticity provides a scientific basis for adopting a growth mindset. And when educators model and teach effective learning strategies, students experience academic gains, which in turn support the process of sustaining a growth mindset to persist even through progressively more difficult learning tasks (Hattie & Anderman, 2020).

These concepts are at the foundation of our work in developing the BrainSMART® programs for improving teaching, learning, and leading through the innovative applications of mind, brain, and education science. Some 165,000 educators around the world over the past two decades have studied these programs through pioneering master's and educational specialist degree programs, doctoral minors, and live professional development events. A key part of these programs has always been developing the learning mindsets that support higher levels of academic and life achievement. This has been achieved in part through the combination of explicitly teaching learners about brain plasticity and *malleable intelligence* (the concept that they can become functionally smarter through effort) and by modeling and teaching specific learning strategies that help them experience higher levels of success.

A hallmark of our approach is including many methods that educators can use "as is" or modify for their practice. This comes from the finding that, in professional development, it is the experience of using a new method in the classroom that makes a positive difference for teachers rather than only learning about a new belief system. As Thomas Guskey (2002) states, teachers experience the most significant changes in their attitudes and beliefs *after* they begin using a new practice and observe the positive effect on student learning. We developed this formula to represent this dynamic:

Mindset + Methods = Growth

The *mindset* in the formula refers to the learners' set of assumptions and beliefs about their potential to learn and grow. We define *potential* as "the neurocognitive capacity for acquiring the knowledge, skills, and attitudes to achieve a higher level of performance in any domain" (Conyers & Wilson, 2015a, p. 4). This definition connects well with the idea that functional or successful intelligence, defined as "one's ability to succeed in life," can be improved (Sternberg, 1999, pp. 292–293; Sternberg, 2018). Mindset can be the engine of motivation (Hattie & Anderman, 2020). When we assume that we can make progress through effort and the use of effective strategies, we are motivated to invest more energy in the learning process. The growth mindset also keeps us going in the face of difficulties and setbacks, as such occurrences can be regarded as feedback telling us we need to use different strategies, ask for help, or invest more time and effort to achieve the desired results.

The *methods* in the formula represents a suite of learning and teaching strategies, skills, lesson ideas, and frameworks, such as those presented throughout this book, for improving learning. As the sum of these components, *growth* refers to ever-increasing levels of knowledge and skills over time. The three elements in this formula work together in a positive feedback loop.

Learning, Teaching, and Mindsets

When I (Donna) first became a teacher and then a school psychologist many years ago, I encountered countless students from across the continuum of socioeconomic status who appeared to be bored, disengaged, and disinterested in school, although I had no doubt they had the potential to succeed. Some of the students I met had experienced circumstances that affected their learning ability at school, such as living in poverty or moving frequently and having to acclimate to new schools. However, many students I encountered had none of these issues yet seemed to feel disconnected from school and generally without hope for succeeding academically, much less enjoying their educational experiences. What became clear was that all of these students could greatly benefit from having what we now know as a growth mindset.

At the same time, I knew colleagues like myself who were working hard with the tools we had to try to motivate students to learn. I found that these educators, like those we have since met around the world, wanted their students to become the best they could be. Through experience, we have learned that it is critically important to build the belief that everyone can and will learn under the right conditions. To create those conditions, we need to build growth mindsets among every stakeholder in education, from students to policymakers.

By modeling some key beliefs, knowledge, and methods in many live workshops, we have witnessed positive transformational changes in educators. Many of the successful methods we use are described in this book, and some are modeled through examples of the positive impact that graduates have been achieving in their classrooms and schools. For example, Carol, a middle school teacher, reports that what she learned in the graduate program "has given me the confidence to challenge myself as well as my students as learners and made me a good role model for them. [It] gave me confidence to speak up about what is right for each student. [I] feel more professional than before. I truly hope I never feel like I am finished learning—this is a gift I want to give my students as well—there's always more they can learn" (Germuth, 2012, p. 22). Carol truly embodies a growth mindset to keep learning as she passes this most important of gifts on to her students.

Our experience has been that when educators incorporate these various methods into their classrooms—such as learning joyfully in groups, participating in "brain breaks" and focused attention practices, and adapting and applying creative methods as appropriate for their students and content—they blossom. We have often commented at the end of a multiday event about how the colors educators wear have changed over the days, going from blacks, dark blues, and browns on the first day of the workshop to yellows, reds, and purples by the last day. It is as if the attendees have been set free to learn, develop, and grow in a safe, lively, and engaging place. In essence, we think that many begin to believe in themselves as learners in new and powerful ways!

In our workshops and online studies, educators have opportunities to grapple with new concepts and grow new knowledge and skills as we work to assist with the development of a mindset that is powered to learn. We find in this process that we, too, learn from the educators we teach. We try to help others avoid falling into the trap of trying to be perfect, which is not only impossible but debilitating to the ability to sustain a growth mindset when learning or teaching. As educators, we must embolden ourselves to break away from the images we are bombarded with in modern culture to be perfect in every way.

We also encourage educators to be open to thinking about what may yet be unknown to them from among the ideas, knowledge, and methods we teach and to embrace those strategies that can help them and their students grow. If you're staying comfortable and not pushing yourself to the edges of discomfort occasionally, you may find that you are not growing.

I (Donna), for example, came face-to-face with my own discomfort as I began practicing yoga with a goal of becoming more flexible and stronger and to establish good habits for maximum well-being in later life. Osteoporosis appears to run in the women of my family. Through exercise and nutritional habits, I have reversed the loss of bone mass in my hips, but my most recent scan indicated decreasing bone mass in my spine. I decided to engage in more stringent exercise. In addition to increasing my resistance training at the gym and adding more steps on my walks, for the first time in my life, I made a commitment to practice yoga.

Starting this regimen while I was writing this book gave me a great opportunity to reflect on my mindset. I admit that when I started yoga in late October, I did not feel positive about my chances for enjoying and sticking with it. It was unfamiliar to me, and I felt stiff, weak, and not very fluid in my movements. Part of the problem was that I was trying to be perfect (the no-no we spoke of earlier, right?). Although my instructors advised me to be less judgmental about my progress as a beginner, I was concerned about making mistakes, even though I knew that mistakes have been found to grow brain connections (as we will discuss in Chapter 2).

I continued practicing yoga, even if only for brief periods almost every day and taking group lessons when possible. As I write this in early March, I can say that by putting myself out there and continuing with yoga, I now feel more flexible and a bit stronger, and I have learned to do a good number of fundamental moves. In essence, I have applied my training, practice, and constructive feedback from my instructors to hone my technique and make incremental gains over time. Through my efforts, I have learned an important skill set that will have ongoing benefits as I continue to mature. Although it will take some time to see positive changes in my bone scans, I hope that the methods I am deploying to build my bones naturally will have positive results in coming years. I'm developing a belief that I can learn and grow my physical skills more than I've believed I could in the past.

Support for a Lifelong Learning Journey

As educators, our objective is to teach children about the benefits of embracing new learning experiences. Whatever we have as cultural values for our youth, all parents want their children to be able to learn across the contexts that society and families hold dear. For example, within a 24-hour news cycle on television, we viewed anxious English teens weeping because they had failed to get into the top universities they had chosen, a 16-year-old boy "shadowing" his father so he could learn how to build cabinets like his dad, and a child sitting at a desk writing her first poem. These three instances represent different values, but in each example, learning is at the core.

Today, perhaps more than ever before, students need to prepare for lives and careers in which they will be constantly facing new learning challenges. One of the top trending skill sets for the future of students now in school is "active learning and learning strategies," according to *The Future of Jobs Report* from the World Economic Forum (2018). Creativity, initiative, critical thinking, flexibility, and complex problem solving will be especially prized among tomorrow's workers, who will need to adapt continually to demands for new skills, especially as job-hopping becomes more commonplace. Guy Berger, an economist with LinkedIn who studied the career paths of 3 million college graduates, points to a study that showed millennials who graduated from 2006 to 2010 were on track to surpass four job changes by the age of 32 (Long, 2016). Berger cites two potential reasons: (1) millennials feel more restless in their careers than previous generations, and (2) employers may regard workers as more disposable. "The best advice I can give anyone is to think about acquiring skills and knowledge that can easily be transferred from one place to another," he says (para. 13).

With this advice in mind, it seems critically important that people discover their tremendous potential to learn throughout their lives and to believe in themselves, believe that they can succeed in learning. This is why, in addition to an emphasis on the development of growth mindsets, we focus on principles (see Figure I.1) and practices that are aligned with the reality of what can help students grow and the knowledge and skills they need to thrive today and in the future, including social and emotional learning across intrapersonal, interpersonal, and cognitive domains.

FIGURE I.1
Wilson and Conyers' Seven Principles for Developing and Sustaining Growth Mindsets

7. Focus on progress, not perfection

6. Improve methods

5. Get the feedback needed

Growth Mindsets

4. Set growth goals

1. Understand the mindsets

2. Keep plasticity front of mind

3. Learn with practical optimism

These principles are designed to assist educators to continue to develop their own growth mindsets and support the development of the growth mindsets of their students:
1. Understand the mindsets so that awareness is maintained with regard to which mindset one is engaged in and what impact it has on motivation and performance.
2. Keep plasticity front of mind as a scientific foundation for developing growth mindsets. Understanding that learning changes the brain can increase motivation.
3. Learn with practical optimism as an approach to support a growth mindset through increased engagement, focused energy, and resilience in the face of challenges.
4. Set growth goals and establish targets with a level of challenge that is not too easy or too difficult.
5. Get the feedback needed to continuously improve learning and sustain a growth mindset.
6. Improve methods—like those shared throughout this book—to increase successful learning outcomes and sustain a growth mindset over time.
7. Focus on progress, not perfection, and celebrate incremental gains.

Each chapter of this book offers support for the journey toward success in learning, with practical methods for teaching and learning aligned with a robust body of research.

Chapter 1: Growth and Fixed Mindsets in Education

Discover Dweck's theory on the power of mindsets—the positive effect a growth mindset has on learning and the impact of a fixed mindset that lessens people's chances to succeed. You will be able to learn about your own mindset by taking a quick assessment; be inspired by our graduate, Debra, as you see how the growth mindset is alive and well in her second-grade classroom; and see how Donna, in a special moment of awareness, began to travel the road from a fixed to a growth mindset for growing intelligence. We will discuss our ABC model to examine fixed and growth mindsets in light of the assumptions, behaviors, and consequences of each mindset.

Chapter 2: Growing Neural Networks

Learn how groundbreaking studies show that the human brain changes during learning and is more malleable across the lifespan than scientists once thought. You will discover how current research about the brain's amazing plasticity forms a neuroscientific understanding of the growth mindset, and you will acquire inspiring knowledge about the structure and function of the brain—including four core factors that power brain growth—to share with your students. Furthermore, you can use this knowledge in lessons about the brain and some of the learning strategies it powers that we've been teaching educators for more than 20 years. You and your students will want to keep knowledge about your brilliant brains front of mind to help motivate growth mindsets.

Chapter 3:
Supporting Positive Engagement and Energized Learning

Discover one of the top requests from teachers to further their professional practice: for knowledge and methods for engaging the focused energy and positive emotions of their students to facilitate learning in the classroom. This chapter shares research from the field of positive psychology and discusses how it links to students' self-talk and concepts of themselves as learners. You will learn methods to guide students to become more practically optimistic and resilient in the face of challenges and cope with negative emotions. This chapter presents strategies to teach students to assess the power of their emotions and positive energy for sustaining learning over time. Incorporating physical activity into the school day to enhance student engagement is also discussed.

Chapter 4:
Motivating Growth Mindsets Through Goals and Feedback

Explore how motivation research over the past four decades has yielded some key methods for assisting students to develop growth mindsets. You will discover the importance of setting high expectations for all learners and for guiding students to embrace their potential for setting and successfully reaching challenging goals. Strategies for helping students choose topics of study, providing them with feedback that supports high motivation and builds growth mindsets, praising effort rather than ability, and using growth assessments are shared.

Chapter 5:
Teaching Strategies That Sustain Growth Mindsets

Learn methods to develop learning environments where all students feel they belong, can relate positively, and contribute in productive ways. We discuss the importance of effective instruction and offer examples of content providing students with opportunities to learn through the brain's multiple pathways and through *deliberate practice*. Teaching techniques cover a range of subjects and broad concepts and provide novel approaches students can apply to enhance learning and sustain growth mindsets over time.

*   *   *   *   *

The seven principles detailed in Figure I.1, which will be explored in more detail throughout this book, translate essential findings from mind, brain, and education research into practical applications teachers can use every day in their classrooms to support students in developing growth mindsets. Let's begin this exploration by discovering how a growth mindset can help students make the most of their learning potential.

Growth and Fixed Mindsets in Education

- -

Growth mindset is based on the belief that your basic qualities are things you can cultivate through your efforts, your strategies, and help from others.

> —Carol Dweck, *Mindset: The New Psychology of Success*
> (2016a, p. 7)

Principle 1: *Understand the mindsets* so that awareness is maintained with regard to which mindset one is engaged in and what impact it has on motivation and performance.

Dweck (2019) identifies the distinction between a *fixed mindset*—the belief that intellectual abilities are static and largely unchangeable—and a *growth mindset*—a belief that intellectual abilities are malleable and can be improved with learning through the use of strategies, practice, and effort. Her work demonstrates that whatever type of mindset individuals adopt can have a major impact on their life across a variety of contexts—in school, with family and friends, and in the workplace. A growth mindset provides students with the motivation to succeed academically, since it allows them to see a correlation between their learning efforts, use of effective strategies, and results.

According to Dweck's conceptualization of these terms, people with a fixed mindset view setbacks—like getting a bad grade or losing a tournament—as failure. Having to work hard to achieve a goal is a sign that they are not smart or talented enough to succeed. In other words, "People with a fixed mindset expect ability to show up on its own, before any learning takes place" (2016a, p. 24). Her research suggests that this mindset—which holds that people have a fixed personality, moral character, and level of intelligence—may have a damaging effect on the achievements of both adults and children. People who regard talent as innate typically believe that working hard is a waste of time. Why work hard if you can't improve? Thus, a fixed mindset may prevent individuals from achieving their *potential* in life—or even acknowledging what their true potential might be. Recasting a familiar phrase about the power of effort and determination, Dweck suggests that people with a fixed mindset would finish the saying "If at first you don't succeed" with "you probably don't have the ability" (pp. 9–10).

People with a growth mindset, on the other hand, are more likely to push themselves to learn new things and keep trying until they achieve their goals, since they are more confident that their efforts will lead to success. As Dweck writes, "Important achievements require a clear focus, all-out effort, and a bottomless trunkful of strategies" (2016a, p. 67). Our aim in this text is to provide that trunkful of strategies and techniques derived from our extensive work supporting teachers with practical, evidence-based methods for guiding students to apply a growth mindset, use effective learning strategies, and persist even when learning gets tough.

Dweck identified five contexts in which mindset makes a crucial difference in learning behaviors: challenges, obstacles, effort, criticism, and the success of others. Figure 1.1 (2016a, p. 263) contrasts various learning behaviors across these contexts.

FIGURE 1.1 Growth Mindset Versus Fixed Mindset		
Contexts	**Growth Mindset**	**Fixed Mindset**
Challenges	Faces challenges	Avoids challenges
Obstacles	Keeps going when the going gets tough	Gives up easily and becomes defensive
Effort	Sees effort as essential for achieving mastery	Sees effort as pointless
Criticism	Actively learns from negative but useful feedback	Ignores negative but useful feedback
Success of others	Learns from and is inspired by the success of others	Is threatened by the success of others

Research suggests that mindsets and resultant learning behaviors have consequences on academic results. Over time, "students who have a growth mindset outperform students who hold a fixed mindset on a variety of outcomes" (PERTS, n.d., p. 6). This is especially true in the face of difficulty (Claro, Paunesku, & Dweck, 2016; Romero, Master, Paunesku, Dweck, & Gross, 2014; Yeager & Dweck, 2012). In 2019, the Programme for International Student Assessment (PISA) released its 2018 study results based on a triennial survey of 15-year-old students around the world. For the first time, the PISA study included a section designed to examine mindsets and their possible relationship to student performance. Some of the findings reported were:

> Holding a growth mindset is positively related to better academic performance in almost every education system. This is especially true for 15-year-old students in the United States. Students who disagreed or strongly disagreed with the statement, "Your intelligence is something about you that you can't change very much" scored 58 points higher in reading that students who agreed or strongly agreed with the statement, after accounting for students' and schools' socioeconomic profile (OECD average: 32 score

points higher). (Organisation for Economic Cooperation and Development, 2019)

In a countrywide initiative with data on the academic performance of 10th graders in Chile, Stanford researchers found that "at every socioeconomic level, those who hold more of a growth mindset consistently outperform those who do not—even after holding constant a panoply of socioeconomic and attitudinal factors" (Claro, Paunesku, & Dweck, 2016, p. 4). In another study with a focus on teenagers, students who received growth mindset training (compared to a matched control group who received other lessons) showed significant gains on measures of math and verbal achievement. Additionally, the researchers found that girls who received the growth mindset training reduced the gender gap in mathematics (Good, Aronson, & Inzlicht, 2003).

In a study with college students, Joshua Aronson and colleagues (2002) found that the growth mindset group showed significantly higher grades than students in control groups. The researchers reported that this finding was largely due to the fact that African American students in the growth mindset group showed a sharp increase in the value they placed on schooling and their enjoyment of academic work.

For those who wish to read more about mindsets across various life contexts, see Dweck's book, *Mindset: The New Psychology of Success* (2016a). To keep abreast of ongoing research on mindsets, check out the Mindset Scholars Network at https://mindsetscholarsnetwork.org. For a short TEDx video of Dwek offering a brief introduction, go to https://www.youtube.com/watch?v=J-swZaKN2Ic.

Mindsets in the Classroom

Debra's Story

Developing growth mindsets and teaching students effective methods for gaining knowledge and skills go hand in hand and are central aspects of our work in teacher education. One teacher who learned with us, Debra, taught her 2nd grade students that learning changes the brain and described how effort and good strategies would help them become smarter. Like Carol, the middle school teacher who was quoted in the Introduction, Debra was one of several teachers who participated in an ethnographic study (Germuth, 2012) exploring the impact of brain-based graduate study on their teaching experience. (The names of all teachers included in this study were changed to protect their privacy and that of their students.)

Among the experiences Debra shared was how she explicitly taught students strategies that could help them develop their reading skills. The result of these efforts was what she called "an explosion of growth" in her students' academic achievement in reading in just a matter of months. She attributed this growth to many specific teaching strategies she used in her classroom, such as "thinking stems," where students were asked to indicate what they wondered, inferred, or thought would occur in a particular story they were reading. As part of this process, students blogged about their thoughts, and a network of educators across the world commented on what students wrote. Not only did Debra's students find this activity meaningful and motivating, but it also made them better readers. Of her 23 students, all but five were reading above grade level after she began to use these methods. Over a three-month period, on average the students made gains of five months in their reading levels, representing advances she had not seen her students make previously (Germuth, 2012).

What a Growth Mindset Isn't

Teachers such as Debra know well that having a growth mindset doesn't automatically mean students will achieve academic growth. Even if students believe they can develop their intellectual abilities, without putting in the work and applying strategies to support improvement, a growth mindset may yield limited results. Dweck identifies the problem of having a "false" growth mindset, which occurs when one subscribes to the concept that people can develop their abilities without fully embracing all the components that make those advances possible. Avoid associating the following actions and attributes with a growth mindset:

- *Telling students they can "do anything."* A growth mindset means you are receptive to the idea that you can develop your knowledge and skills, but not every goal is achievable by every person. Telling students they can do whatever they try to do without methods for getting there may give them a false sense that success is easy—and ultimately set them up for failure. A teacher's role is to show students how to develop the necessary skills and access the resources that will be useful to them as they pursue a specific goal. That will be far more effective and meaningful to them than empty platitudes that don't convey what it takes to develop and grow throughout life.
- *Having positive qualities such as open-mindedness or flexibility.* While Dweck observes that these are positive traits, educators should understand that being open-minded is not the same thing as putting in the effort to develop their own abilities and those of their students.
- *Praising effort without linking to other strategies necessary for success.* While it's true that hard work is important to learning, praising someone's effort without tying it to other learning strategies—like focus and perseverance—does not reinforce those necessary connections. The best way for teachers to give feedback is to praise students for hard work and link the praise to the outcome and the strategies they used to get there (Dweck, 2016a, 2016b).

Shifting to a Growth Mindset

Students with a fixed mindset may be more likely to struggle academically in comparison to their counterparts who have a growth mindset. Dweck confirmed this connection in a study she conducted that followed students for two years as they transitioned from elementary school to middle school. Students were asked prior to the study whether they believed intelligence was a fixed trait or something they could develop. Though students in both groups had similar academic records at the start of the study, those with a fixed mindset showed a steady decline in grades over the next two years, while those with a growth mindset did not. Because the transition to middle school is a challenging and stressful time, those with a fixed mindset often feel overwhelmed and consider themselves unequipped for achieving academic success. "With the threat of failure looming," Dweck writes, "students with the growth mindset instead mobilized their resources for learning. They told us that they, too, sometimes felt overwhelmed, but their response was to dig in and do what it takes" (2016a, pp. 57–58).

Motivated by a growth mindset, these students were able to put forth greater effort in the face of academic challenges. Teachers who espouse a growth mindset are in a position to help students increase their motivation, put forth the hard work, and apply useful learning strategies that will lead them to greater academic success. Motivation and effort are two critical components that can drive anyone, including low-performing students, to learn and achieve.

We've worked with many teachers who exhibit a growth mindset through their love of learning. Georgia teacher Melissa Smith shares her commitment to lifelong learning with her students with personal examples, such as her karate lessons, certification in yoga, and research on nutrition and health. Melissa states:

> I share my desire to try and do new things. Sometimes I ask students to teach me things they know, like dance moves or an art skill. I practice what I preach, and they can see that as they watch me try things and think aloud, so they see the process. Sometimes I succeed easily, and at other times,

they see frustration, diligence, and starting over.... I hope that by not just explaining, but by modeling, I can bring light to the fact that all learning is helpful and can impact your life positively by keeping your brain cells active and buzzing with healthy engagement—all while teaching you to be persistent, creative, diligent, and flexible. These skills not only make you employable and healthy, but also resilient and happy. (Personal correspondence, April 2, 2019)

Along the same lines, Donna observed growth mindsets at work in schools in a parish (county) in the Mississippi Delta: After conducting a series of workshops there, I had the pleasure of going into classrooms to observe teachers presenting and facilitating a lesson using knowledge and strategies shared in the workshops. I was amazed and inspired to see every teacher's unique skill as they each shared some of what they had learned from our time together. Most applications were passionate, innovative, and effective at engaging students to learn.

Metacognition and Mindset

One way to assess your understanding of mindsets is to use the tool of *metacognition,* which we define as "thinking about one's thinking with the goal of enhancing learning" (Wilson & Conyers, 2016a, p. 8). Using this essential tool is sometimes understood as taking a step back to observe your thoughts and actions. An important aspect of metacognition is self-awareness, which involves being conscious of various aspects of yourself, including beliefs, emotions, self-talk, and behaviors (see Figure 1.2).

By becoming aware of a fixed mindset when you are confronted with a challenge, it is possible to begin putting in the necessary effort, identifying and applying useful strategies, and persevering to reach your goals. This progression is illustrated by Donna's story about starting yoga, which we shared in the Introduction. Without self-awareness, a more likely response is to react passively. For example, she might have quit yoga early on, thinking that she had waited too long and was just too uncoordinated and inflexible to learn it. She would have given up on herself and missed the opportunity for greater well-being. Instead, by being self-aware, when she noticed that she was saying things to herself like "I just can't do this" or "I'm too old to try. Why should I even try to learn it?," she recognized that a fixed mindset had been triggered, and she consciously set out to apply a growth mindset and commit to the work necessary to continue practicing yoga. Now her messages to herself sound more like: "I can see a little progress here on this hamstring stretch." "What a good workout I had!" "I feel good—the effort was well worth it!"

FIGURE 1.2
Being Aware of Our Mindsets

Am I in a fixed
or growth mindset?

Gaining Insight into Your Mindsets

You can apply metacognition to better understand which type of mindset you have and how this propensity affects your ability to learn and improve. Dweck developed the following statements that can be used as a guide to evaluate whether you have a fixed mindset, a growth mindset, or a combination of the two with regard to intelligence.

- Your intelligence is something very basic about you that you can't change very much.
- You can learn new things, but you can't really change how intelligent you are.
- No matter how much intelligence you have, you can always change it quite a bit.
- You can always substantially change how intelligent you are. (Dweck, 2016a, p. 12)

The first two statements indicate a fixed mindset, whereas the last two reflect a growth mindset. Your "intelligence mindset" is engaged in situations that involve mental ability, such as academics, creative endeavors, reasoning, and problem solving. Mindsets can differ across contexts. For example, a person may be confident about her ability to learn a new language and put in the necessary study and practice to become adept in that domain over time. On the other hand, she believes her struggle with math-related skills is innate. She says, "I don't have the math gene." She exhibits a growth mindset for learning a language and a fixed mindset about developing her understanding of math.

The concepts of growth and fixed mindsets can also be applied to personality, social and emotional intelligence, and creative and athletic abilities (the Appendix includes exercises to explore mindsets aligned with the teaching profession and regarding personality traits). Again, it's possible to have a growth mindset in some areas and a fixed mindset in others. Your "personality mindset" is more relevant in situations that involve personal attributes. If you have a growth personality mindset, for example, you're more likely to learn from negative social situations, whereas a fixed mindset may cause you to dwell on how you were judged (Dweck, 2016a, p. 13).

As an example of applying mindsets more widely, let's return to Donna's experience with yoga: She did not believe in her potential to learn the postures and was fearful of making mistakes. In other words, she had a fixed mindset about learning in that specific area of her life. But her mindset regarding her learning of athletic skills stands in stark contrast to her transformation from a fixed to growth mindset regarding intelligence and academics many years ago. Having these two varying mindsets about two different aspects of her life clearly illustrates that we can embody both growth and fixed mindsets at any one time depending on the context, the amount of time we have put into practice, and other factors.

In our workshops, we describe how people—students and educators alike—have what we call "peaks and valleys" in their mindsets, skills, and knowledge. For the past 30 years, Donna's growth mindset for learning new academic knowledge and skills has been a "peak" because it has been a focus in her life. However, largely due to the fact that she had not taken time to develop as much in the physical exercise domain, she experienced a "valley" in her mindset regarding yoga. Fortunately, through effort, lessons, and practice, she has been delighted to find that she is now developing a growth mindset that has allowed her to improve her yoga abilities. One can climb out of the "valleys" through hard work over time. This example also suggests the value of thinking of mindsets on a continuum rather than as an absolute—with variation across contexts and intensity.

As you read this book, we hope you feel encouraged to embrace improvement across aspects of your life you choose to change while feeling affirmed as you think about the many things you have already accomplished. Be kind to yourself with regard to your mindset in the contexts you choose to explore. We have learned that newfound self-awareness can be the impetus to take on amazing new challenges, conquests, and adventures—changing what was a fixed mindset in specific areas of your life to a growth mindset that will provide you with more satisfaction and fulfillment.

Donna's Lifelong Journey to a Growth Mindset

As a practicing school psychologist in the 1980s, I (Donna) was driven to learn more that could help me support the students I was serving. At the time, I was assessing hundreds of students from prekindergarten through high school who were referred due to academic and behavioral difficulties. I had met many students facing the same challenges when I was a classroom teacher earlier in my career. I had become increasingly more concerned as U.S. standards were set ever higher and the number of students who were unsuccessful at school increased dramatically. At the same time, a common assumption by adults and students was that intelligence was fixed, which was accepted as an explanation for declining academic performance. Furthermore, a major focus of school psychology at the time was on intelligence testing and labeling and not on supporting more effective teaching and learning practices. In that context, when I learned of the hope and passion embodied in psychologist Reuven Feuerstein's belief that intelligence is dynamic and malleable, I was hopeful that his approach might help me assist many of the students who had lost hope of succeeding in school. His findings are reflected in the work of a small group of other psychologists, such as Robert Sternberg, who also espoused a belief in intelligence as dynamic and changeable rather than fixed. Their thinking rocked my world when—in one moment in the spring of 1989, listening to Feuerstein's keynote address at a conference at the University of Tennessee—I realized that we have a choice about whether we believe that learning grows intelligence or that intelligence remains fixed throughout life.

Thinking about these two views of intelligence and learning with children I wanted to help, I came to realize that many students I assessed had a view of their intelligence as fixed and, thus, had lost hope of succeeding in school. Even when they had high IQ scores, many of the students seemed shut down and fearful of making mistakes. This was in direct contrast to students who thought they could become smarter through hard work, practice, and inquiry, when necessary. These students tended to do the work it took to do well at school. They were more likely to respond to challenges by engaging in behaviors that helped them learn, such as using strategies to solve problems and seeking out help when necessary.

After Feuerstein's address, I took advantage of the opportunity to speak with him. I wanted to learn more about his conceptions of dynamic intelligence with an intention to use his methods in my practice, but to be honest, I couldn't help but wonder if I was up to this learning challenge. I confessed my qualms when we met. He asked me if I knew what a ricochet was. Then he said gently, "Donna, as you teach it, you will better learn it. It will come back to you!" In one moment, with a simple sentence, a teacher helped me choose a very different course for my life. Leaving the conference to return home, I continued to think about my beliefs concerning intelligence. Hearing that I, an ordinary person with no special gifts or talents, might actually be able to grow my intelligence and use it to help others was a dream come true. I began to consider new possibilities.

Inspired by role models and growth-minded theorists whose work I had the opportunity to read and who I'd met, I began a journey of research, development, and implementation and decided to go back to school. Two years after attending that fateful conference, I began the PhD program in educational psychology at the University of Oklahoma to study motivation and cognition. It was during my studies diving into the topic of motivation that I began to explore Dweck's work. Looking back, I realize that I went from a belief in fixed intelligence to a belief that as we learn, we grow our functional intelligence. First, I learned I had a choice. Then, over time, I continued to learn and develop a growth mindset, knowing that I was growing my intelligence.

Indeed, our mindsets influence our journeys. Upon completing my doctoral studies in 1994, I actualized my goal to become a university professor and chairperson at the University of Detroit Mercy and went on to complete postdoctoral studies overseas with Feuerstein. This move took me far from family and friends I knew and loved in my home state of Oklahoma, but I considered my move a big adventure!

In 1998, while in Chicago at a conference on learning, teaching, and the brain, I met Marcus Conyers, who became the love of my life. A handsome man hailing from Cambridge, England, he impressed me with his knowledge and teaching skills. His focus was on teaching the science of brain plasticity and modeling practical methods for increasing student learning—a powerful combination. When I had a chance to observe him teach, I noticed how engaged teachers and administrators were. We talked a lot over the next months, and I learned that he, too, embodied a belief that virtually all people could become functionally smarter given the right conditions. As time went on, we fell in love, married, and have continued to enjoy living, teaching, and learning together.

Our purpose in including this personal story goes beyond giving readers the opportunity to "meet the authors"; it's to offer a firsthand illustration that it is possible to change your mindset. Systematically taking the time to step back, review the challenge, and choose the mindset that will best support you can be a powerful opportunity to move forward.

Dweck (2016a) proposes that it is possible to develop a growth mindset by modeling the behavior of others. As I did in my life, you can observe how people you know or are learning about embody the concepts of improving their knowledge and skills as they take on obstacles and challenges in their lives. Is there a way you can emulate one of those individuals so that you can similarly grow the knowledge and skills you desire?

What has been most inspiring to us around the world—from our work with teachers in Asia to our presentations with educators from across Australia, New Zealand, and South Africa, to our keynotes and presentations in the Middle East and Europe and across the United States and Canada—is that educators have a tremendous opportunity to help all students reach more of their potential by explicitly teaching using the Mindset + Methods = Growth formula. Looking back over our lives in light of living a belief in Dweck's concept of growth mindsets, we have come to believe that perhaps more than anything else, our growth mindsets—especially having to do with learning, career, and love—have transformed our lives for the better.

Three Strategies to Foster Growth Mindsets in Your Classroom

To foster growth mindsets in your classroom:

- *Introduce the concept of a growth mindset to your students by explaining that their beliefs in their abilities to learn new knowledge and skills can help them succeed even when the learning gets tough.* The strategies and techniques shared in Chapters 2–5 will help reinforce that message throughout the school year.
- *Apply a metacognitive approach to your own mindset in your teaching practice.* Reflect on situations in your past and current practice where you have applied a growth mindset to gain mastery of new knowledge and skills.
- *Look for opportunities to apply our formula—Mindset + Methods = Growth—in your teaching practice.* By maintaining a growth mindset about your students' learning potential and applying learning strategies and techniques like those shared in this book, you can guide your students to continually develop new knowledge and skills—and experience a positive, upward learning spiral of success!

Teacher-Tested Technique:
Thinking About Mindsets Using the ABC Model

We can compare the two mindsets—fixed and growth—by using our ABCs—assumptions, behaviors, and consequences—to determine how we think about our capacity to learn, achieve, and succeed. Using the ABC model for this exercise, we are better able to understand the impact of our mindsets (see Figure 1.3). What we think about our potential to succeed (our assumptions) influences how we act (our behaviors), and how we act leads to certain outcomes (consequences) (Conyers & Wilson, 2015a).

FIGURE 1.3
The ABC Model Applied to Mindsets in Education

	Fixed Mindset Approach	Growth Mindset Approach
Assumptions	Our abilities and intellect are fixed and innate, largely the product of genetics.	Our abilities and intellect are malleable and can be improved.
Behaviors	In classrooms and schools, a few students identified as having high levels of innate talent are provided a conducive environment to allow them to flourish. Fewer opportunities are offered to those assessed as having less innate talent.	Educators create opportunities for students across the spectrum of academic achievement to develop their knowledge, skills, and abilities. Students are supported with feedback that encourages effort, the use of effective learning strategies, and requests for help when needed. Progress, not perfection, is the goal.
Consequences	Many students are not given opportunities to learn and grow.	Students across the spectrum realize higher levels of achievement, and teachers are supported with effective professional development.

The Fixed Mindset Approach

Assumptions.

- Our abilities and intellect are fixed and innate, largely the product of genetics.
- Special talents are obvious early in life.
- These talents and gifts develop with minimal effort.
- Talent is limited to only a few.

Behaviors. A common practice in many schools and districts is to identify a small percentage of individuals perceived to have high levels of innate talent and provide a conducive environment to allow them to flourish. Fewer opportunities are offered to those assessed as having less innate talent. For example, many students who start school behind their peers in reading do not receive the support they need to catch up and read at grade level.

Consequences. Many students are not given opportunities to learn and grow. They internalize the misconception that they lack the capacity to learn, to excel, and to succeed. This reduces their efforts to strive to improve their skills and abilities. Fixed mindsets may have negative ramifications for those identified as gifted and talented as well. If they embrace the assumption that their innate gifts will develop naturally with minimal effort, they may fail to develop their true potential by not putting in the hard work necessary to excel. Thus, the full consequences may be a massive achievement gap in their potential and actual achievement.

Marcus sees fixed mindsets in action when presenting at live events: I'll ask for a show of hands of people who lack the talent for art. Often a large percentage of the audience raise their hands. Then I ask them how old they were when they discovered they couldn't "do" art. The typical range of responses is between age six and nine. Some people will share what led to their discovery—perhaps an offhanded comment from a teacher or the realization that their drawings were never chosen for display in class.

Sometimes an individual will respond, "My brother was the artist in the family, and I was the athlete"—as if we can only be one or the other, as if because of our childhood interests and less-than-successful first efforts, some doors are closed to us forever. The same responses may have been given if I'd asked, "How many of you are naturally good at math?" or "Do you think of yourself as a good presenter?" And yet, the skills at the foundations of these endeavors—creativity, analytical abilities, problem solving, and effective communication—can all be learned and improved.

We have found that when teachers learn about brain plasticity and human potential, it can change their assumptions and teaching behaviors dramatically, which can then change the consequences for students. Let's revisit Debra, the 2nd grade teacher from our ethnographic study, who provides some enlightenment on this subject. Before completing her graduate degree program, Debra provided enrichment only to those students who tested into the gifted program. She has changed that strategy since earning her degree, based on the realization that all students have the potential to be more effective at learning. Rather than basing enrichment opportunities on assessment scores, she provides as many meaningful and enriching activities as possible to all of her students, using strategies and suggestions she has learned as part of her teaching education (Germuth, 2012).

The Growth Mindset Approach
Assumptions.

- We have tremendous untapped potential, the product of the combination of genetic traits and environment.
- Our intellect and abilities are malleable and improvable.
- Our intellect and abilities can be enhanced through conscious effort over time.
- The vast majority of people can get good or better at the abilities of their choosing with learning and practice.

Behaviors. Teachers, schools, and districts focus on creating opportunities for students across the entire spectrum of academic achievement to develop their knowledge, skills, and abilities to a high level. The focus is not on perfection, but rather on trying new things that may possibly work better for more students more of the time. When BrainSMART graduate Leanne Caparro (formerly Maule) was a high school teacher, she was committed to holding all students, not just high achievers, to ambitious standards. As one example, her 9th grade remedial English students acted out the same scenes from *Romeo and Juliet* as gifted students in the same grade—but instead of performing the scenes in traditional fashion, they adapted them into modern contexts of their own creation. This enabled students to increase and demonstrate their understanding of Shakespeare's language by putting it into their own words (Maule, 2009). In her current post as an instructional coach in Hartwell, Georgia, Leanne guides teachers to use best practices, including measuring student growth. This focus underscores the importance of maintaining a growth mindset regarding learning gains for all students.

Consequences. Many more students realize higher levels of achievement. More confident of their abilities to improve with effort, they put in the hard work necessary to do so—and receive encouragement from others (teachers, parents, coaches) in their endeavors. They also learn and employ useful strategies to help achieve their ambitious goals.

The conclusion that can be drawn from Debra's and Leanne's stories is that effective instruction and support for learning can help all students—especially those who arrive unprepared to "do school"—catch up to their peers. These stories point to the potential for teachers to have a significant impact on students' intelligence and achievement. Teachers with a growth mindset—those who believe that intelligence is malleable or changeable—can model this mindset in the classroom and foster the growth mindset among their students, leading to greater student motivation and effort. Working from this mindset, students can become functionally smarter. In the process of assisting students to become smarter, the teachers you are meeting in this book are increasing their enjoyment of teaching and experiencing personal growth.

The power of a growth mindset to enhance teaching and learning puts into practice the conclusion from the American Psychological Association that "thinking about intelligence as changeable and malleable, rather than stable and fixed, results in greater academic achievement, especially for people whose groups bear the burdens of negative stereotypes about their intelligence" (2015, para. 1).

Growing Neural Networks

As people acquire knowledge, there are significant changes in their brain activity, brain structure, or both that complement the rapid increase in processing speed and effort needed to use the acquired knowledge.

—National Academies of Sciences, Engineering, and Medicine
(2018, p. 63)

Principle 2: *Keep plasticity front of mind* as a scientific foundation for developing growth mindsets. Understanding that learning changes the brain can increase motivation.

In our interactions with educators, we have observed again and again that they are eager to increase their knowledge about how the brain changes as a result of learning. Teachers enjoy using their newfound knowledge about the brain not only to become more effective in enhancing the learning of their students but also to become more effective learners themselves. In essence, educators are inspired to discover exciting new findings about the brain.

Learning about the brain fascinates people of all ages. We recommend that you consider facilitating lessons on the brain in your classroom; sample lessons are included in the Teacher-Tested Techniques section at the end of this chapter. Many of our graduates across all grade levels and content areas have done so with great results and for good reason: When students learn that their brain is a powerful tool that grows new connections when they learn, this discovery is extremely motivating. It is especially critical information for students who do not view themselves as being capable. By recognizing how their brain has the capacity to change and make them smarter, they become more emotionally invested in their learning, leading to greater engagement. As affective neuroscientist Mary Helen Immordino-Yang (2016) points out, an emotional connection is essential to learning. She stresses that emotions are where learning begins and makes a strong point that "it is literally neurobiologically impossible to think deeply about things that you don't care about" (Lahey, 2016). Virtually everyone we have met around the world cares about learning about the brain.

Connecting Brain Science to a Growth Mindset

Learning about the brain's capacity to change is important in helping educators further develop a growth mindset and sustain it over time. One of our graduates, classroom teacher Miriam, finds this to be incredibly motivating. "One of the most fascinating things [we learned] was [about] brain plasticity—the finding that the brain is pretty elastic even as you get old" (Germuth, 2012, p. 28). Discovering how learning changes the brain and keeping this knowledge front of mind can serve as a basis for educators to guide students in developing growth mindsets.

Miriam refers to studies that show evidence of synaptic development at work in brain scans of medical students studying for exams, musicians engaged in rigorous practice, and cab drivers learning to navigate the streets of London (Draganski et al., 2006; Gaser & Schlaug, 2003; Woollett & Maguire, 2011). This research identifies visible changes in areas of the brain associated with memory, spatial reasoning, and problem solving. These findings support a conceptualization of intelligence as malleable and dynamic.

Given this emerging understanding of malleable intelligence, the acceptance of a growth mindset versus a fixed mindset is becoming more common in some academic circles. With reference to this body of research, a recent paper from the Harvard Graduate School of Education affirms that the brain's architecture continually adapts as we learn and points out that "while both beliefs [growth and fixed mindsets] are still commonly held among students... belief in a growth mindset is scientifically accurate, whereas belief in a fixed mindset is a misconception" (2015, p. 2).

Exploring Brain Waves and Mindsets

It turns out that whether someone has a fixed or growth mindset shows up in differences in brain waves. While people with both mindsets answered difficult questions and got feedback, Dweck and other researchers at Columbia University conducted brain scans. The researchers found that those with a fixed mindset were only interested when the feedback reflected on their ability. Their brain waves showed them paying close attention when they were told whether their answers were right or wrong. But when they were presented with information that could help them learn, there was no sign of interest (Dweck, 2016a, p. 18).

In fact, the researchers detected little interest among subjects with a fixed mindset in even finding out the right answer. Only those with a growth mindset paid attention "to information that could stretch their knowledge. Only for them was learning a priority" (p. 18).

Mistakes and Mindsets in the Brain

In another brain study yielding information about mindsets, Michigan State University's Jason Moser and colleagues found that those who believe in malleable intelligence respond to mistakes differently than people who believe intelligence is fixed. In the study, each participant wore a cap that recorded electrical activity in the brain. The apparatus recorded the brain's almost instantaneous response to making a mistake, which consists of two signals: an indication of the brain's awareness that something has gone wrong and an attempt to correct the mistake.

The study showed that participants who thought they could learn from their mistakes—those with a growth mindset—actually did better after making a misstep. Their brains reacted differently, producing a larger signal the second time. This signal says, "I know I've made a mistake, so I'll pay more attention." The research shows that these two groups of people—one with fixed mindsets and the other with growth mindsets—are fundamentally different. People who think they can learn from their mistakes have brains that pay more attention to mistakes, so they are better able to correct them (Association for Psychological Science, 2011).

Your Brain at Work

Thus, a firm foundation for developing a growth mindset begins with a basic understanding of the physiology of the human brain. The brain is the control center in charge of all our functions, which includes everything from controlling our heart rate and breathing to receiving and interpreting input from our senses to facilitating thought and experiencing emotions. As you might expect from the organ that controls virtually everything in the human mind and body, the brain is complex. It powers our ability to learn, our capacity to increase our knowledge and skills, and the way our temperament manifests. The knowledge we share about the brain in the first part of this chapter is helpful to include as appropriate for your students when guiding them to understand more about their brilliant brains.

Neural Plasticity

Scientists use the term *neuroplasticity* (or *neural plasticity*) to describe how the structure of the brain changes over the course of an individual's lifetime. These changes occur as a result of thoughts and actions as well as sensory input (what we see, hear, taste, smell, and touch). In fact, there is conclusive proof, discernable by the human eye on MRI scans, that neural connections in the brain are actually strengthened through learning, as reinforced by such activities as practice and repetition. The neural networks associated with learning activities and focused attention actually grow denser and larger, leading to what neurologist Majid Fotuhi describes as "enhanced brain performance" (2013, p. 4). With this in mind, we share strategies in this book that help to develop attention, memory, and metacognition—key elements of *executive function* essential for what we call driving your brain (ASCD, 2018; Wilson & Conyers, 2016a, 2020).

Fotuhi further explains that "when you learn something new, you create new synapses... when you continue to use those synapses, you strengthen them." This is a process known as *synaptogenesis*, whereby "measurable structural changes in the brain" can happen in as little as a few weeks by practicing new knowledge and skills (2013, p. 113). Understanding the process of synaptogenesis is quite encouraging, as it replaces the disheartening premise that a student doesn't have the mental capacity to learn a lesson with the more hopeful and actionable conclusion that he simply hasn't learned it yet. As an elementary music teacher who studied with us said, "Everyone has the plasticity to grow. If you're interested in music, you might not become Yo-Yo Ma, but if you start out as a one, you can work to become a two, and then a three. Plasticity means that everyone has the potential to achieve. Students can make themselves smarter by their own effort" (Wilson & Conyers, 2013b).

Four Core Factors That Power Brain Growth

Several factors work to power neurocognitive synergy in a manner that supports learning, recall, and the incremental and ongoing development of knowledge and skills. Essentially, these factors can be seen as the machinery that is the basis for life itself and learning that occurs across the lifespan.

Fotuhi (2013) refers to the "Core 4" of growing your brain as: (1) neurogenesis (increasing the number of brain cells); (2) synaptogenesis (adding synaptic connections); (3) myelination (bolstering neuronal connections; and (4) angiogenesis (blood flow in the body and brain).

Neurogenesis

The most basic operating units of the brain are neurons—nerve cells that transmit signals in the form of electrical impulses. For much of the 20th century, many scientists believed *neurogenesis*, or the creation of new neurons, occurred only in young brains. They viewed adulthood as a period of steady, inevitable neurological decline. However, a major breakthrough occurred in the 1980s when researchers discovered that the brains of adult songbirds formed new neurons as they learned new songs (Riddle & Lichtenwalner, 2007). That research led to a realization, confirmed by subsequent research, that other living creatures—up to and including humans—could likewise form new neurons as a part of the learning process.

Teachers have told us that the information we have shared about neurogenesis and brain plasticity in our programs has had a positive impact in their classrooms. For example, Brianne sees brain plasticity as "an important concept for educators to understand because they need to be aware of the fact that everyone has the ability to learn.... Educators and leaders will also benefit as they recognize learning never stops, regardless of an individual's age" (Germuth, 2012, p. 12).

Synaptogenesis

The formation of neural connections between the cells is known as *synaptogenesis*. The more activity that is transmitted through those networks, the stronger the connections. However, when these connections are not reinforced with regular stimuli, they are weakened and ultimately eliminated—hence the often-given advice to "use it or lose it." Decreases in those networks are referred to as *pruning*; while such a term may seem to imply that this is a negative thing, it's actually a natural and useful process that ensures that the brain operates efficiently. Both synaptogenesis and pruning are behind the structural changes that encode learning and memories in the brain. These processes are essential to the continual development of the skills and knowledge required to accomplish the goals you set for yourself.

Experience-dependent synaptogenesis refers to the formation of synaptic connections that occur in response to our experiences and environments. These connections don't just form naturally but rather are a direct result of what we learn through our senses and activities and our thinking processes. The more we think about or do something, the stronger these connections become. Experience-dependent synaptogenesis occurs when children crack the reading code, master a mathematical equation, expand their vocabulary, become proficient at a musical instrument, or learn a new dance move. It happens because we decide to learn something new, commit the time and effort to doing so, and tap into various resources—such as a good teacher, coach, or pertinent information—to facilitate our learning.

Myelination

The brain consists of both gray matter, which is primarily neurons, and "white matter," or myelin, which is composed of fats, protein, and water. Myelin is produced by glial cells and interspersed among neurons to insulate and support neural connections. It serves as an electrical conductor that increases the speed and strength of the impulses transmitted among neurons. Adequate *myelination* supports healthy brain and body functioning; conversely, a breakdown in the myelination process, referred to as *demyelination* in the brain and spinal cord, is a factor in multiple sclerosis (MS) and other diseases that cause nervous system degeneration.

Angiogenesis

Blood vessels supply oxygen and nutrients to the body and brain. *Angiogenesis*, which is the development of new blood vessels, helps maintain the blood supply to the brain. A healthy diet and regular exercise enhance the development of new blood vessels for peak functioning of the *body–brain* system.

Four Teaching Methods for Developing Brain Connections

The following four teaching methods illustrate our Mindset + Methods = Growth formula and are among the many ways for developing growth mindsets that we share throughout this book. In our live events with teachers, after we share basic information about brain plasticity, we focus on the following ideas for supporting learning and brain change, based broadly on the work of Michael Merzenich, a well-known leader in the study of neuroplasticity whose book, *Soft-Wired* (2013), we recommend for further enlightenment on this subject.

Novelty

Keep students' learning experiences fresh. Adding variety to lessons, group learning events, presentations, and assessments helps keep the brain engaged. As you read through this book, you will notice many methods that our graduates enjoy sharing with students, partially for the purpose of creating more lively classrooms to facilitate active learning of the knowledge and skills they teach. For example, think of a conference you may have attended that consisted of a series of lectures, some with a monotone presentation style. A few weeks later, how much were you able to recall and apply? Think of another learning experience where the presenter was passionate about sharing relevant research, modeled new strategies, and then provided opportunities for you to share with a partner and try these strategies out for the first time. Was your recall significantly better? Were you able to apply more of the material you learned?

Challenge

Use learning goals that are attainable yet challenging. In the same way that muscle growth requires lifting heavier weights or increased repetitions, the brain needs greater challenges to stimulate the growth of new connections or strengthen existing connections. This is an example of where *formative (growth) assessment* is important so that useful growth goals can be determined. This helps educators find out where students are and what reasonable growth goals might be engaging and appropriately challenging. Over the course of time, as students overcome difficulties in completing challenging learning tasks, they have the opportunity to develop grit and self-confidence.

Practice

Give learners a chance to have enough practice distributed over time to create learning that lasts. There is an expression in neuroscience: "Practice makes cortex" (Duerden & Laverdure-Dupont, 2008). This is an important concept to keep front of mind as you create learning environments that develop growth mindsets. Students need time to practice new skills, such as reading, writing, solving math problems, or achieving mastery in any content area. The key is to "practice smart." In other words, to focus practice where it is needed most—on areas that have not yet been mastered.

Feedback

Provide students with timely information about how they are progressing toward completing a learning goal. Beneficial feedback is actionable, transparent, specific and personalized, ongoing, and consistent (Wiggins, 2012). John Hattie and Helen Timperley (2007) state that effective feedback must answer three key questions: "What is the goal?", "What progress is being made with regard to the goal?", and "What actions need to be taken to make better progress?" Effective feedback can be motivational and result in helping students invest more effort to reach their goals, thus helping them develop a growth mindset for learning. Chapter 4 provides more information on how to give students feedback that helps them develop a growth mindset.

Applying the Teaching Methods in the Classroom

Classroom teacher Diane Dahl credits an understanding of brain plasticity and the learning of methods such as the four described previously for "revolutionizing" daily teaching strategies

> My class no longer sits for long periods of time. When we do sit, the students often choose where they want to sit. I give students more choices in their lessons. We use more senses in daily work—and less paper. Students have a more interesting and interactive school day. (Wilson & Conyers, 2013a, p. 8)

In essence, Ms. Dahl is creating an environment and innovative learning experiences that can develop growth mindsets and effective acquisition of new knowledge and skills by her students as she enjoys teaching more than ever before.

Virtual Reality

If you are familiar with video games, you can likely identify how game developers use these strategies to captivate the interest of people across different ages and stages of life. We often hear teachers say that some students have limited motivation and drive to master curriculum material. However, these same students will invest hours in mastering video games that have the *novelty* of being new, a *challenge* that is just beyond current performance level, the need for *practice* in order to make progress, and ongoing *feedback* in terms of points and scores, as well as the rewards of moving to higher, more challenging levels.

Learning Across the Lifespan

Here are two examples of the power of learning across the lifespan: The first comes from a classroom I (Marcus) visited after leading professional development on methods to support brain-based learning for educators in the district. As I walked into the classroom of 25 students, my eyes were drawn to one student in particular. He had a beaming smile and was so eager to speak that he could scarcely stay in his seat. With a nod of assent from his teacher, he bounded to the front of the room and gave me a high-five. He thanked me for sharing information with his teacher about how the brain changes as it learns and how students can learn more effectively. This student, who I later learned had been held back a grade, was so excited to discover that he could get smarter and smarter by applying effective strategies. This and a host of other feedback we have received from educators and students over the years have confirmed the importance of developing a positive view about the brain's capacity to change as a result of learning. It also reinforces the positive impact of the use of teaching and learning strategies, as well as other methods for increasing academic achievement and developing growth mindsets.

My second example involves my mother, who asked me several years ago how she could keep her brain youthful. In my experience growing up in Cambridge, England, it was rare for parents to ask their children for input, so before she changed her mind, I rushed to tell her how we share four methods to support and enhance learning. Using these methods helped my mother pursue a lifelong dream—painting. She had always wanted to paint, but as a child in school, she was told she had no artistic talent and could not learn it. But taking my advice many years later, she took lessons, practiced her technique, and sought feedback from her teacher and fellow painters. A couple years later, we were delighted to receive the cover of an English art magazine featuring her creative and award-winning oil paintings.

Three Strategies for Supporting Brain-Powered Growth Mindsets

To support brain-powered growth mindsets:

- *Introduce your students to the concept of their brain's amazing plasticity as a scientific foundation for developing growth mindsets.* We have found that when students understand that learning changes the brain, their motivation to engage in learning, overcome learning challenges, and develop growth mindsets increases.
- *Incorporate the concepts of novelty, challenge, practice, and feedback into your teaching* to take full advantage of opportunities to engage students' brains in learning.
- *After introducing growth mindsets and brain plasticity to your students, guide them to use the strategies included throughout this book.* As you link growth mindsets to teaching students strategies, you are applying our formula—Mindset + Methods = Growth—in your teaching practice.

Teacher-Tested Techniques: Teaching Students About Their Amazing Brains

In our approach, we have long supported educators to guide students in developing a belief through learning about brain plasticity that they can learn most anything if they are willing to put in effort and apply appropriate strategies (ASCD, 2018; Conyers & Wilson, 2015a; Wilson & Conyers, 2016a, 2018, 2020). Many educators with whom we have worked, from preK through college, enjoy inspiring students with knowledge about their amazing brain plasticity, some key brain facts, and study strategies such as those offered later in this chapter.

Their students are motivated to put more effort into their learning once they understand how powerful their brains are. We have found that when children and youth learn that they have the potential to succeed at school and in life, this knowledge is truly a game changer. This is consistent with three factors in the framework for increasing social and emotional learning from the Collaborative for Academic, Social, and Emotional Learning (Durlak, Weissberg, Dymnicki, Taylor, & Schellinger, 2011): self-confidence, self-efficacy, and recognition of strengths.

Lisa Blackwell and colleagues (2007) reported similar findings in their investigation of 7th graders and math achievement. During the eight sessions of the study, two groups were taught study skills. One of the two groups, the "growth mindset group," was taught a workshop beginning with an article that fascinated them, "You Can Grow Your Intelligence: New Research Shows the Brain Can Be Developed Like a Muscle" (National Association of Independent Schools, 2008). They continued to learn about how they could apply a growth mindset in their schoolwork. The second group, which was taught lessons about memory, showed no improvement in math, and eventually their performance declined. These students appeared to lack the motivation to put the study skills they had learned into practice. In the growth mindset group, the students' teachers were able to see positive changes in motivation for the students. They stated that these students were more engaged with their schoolwork and were putting more effort into their assignments and learning.

Following are some popular lesson ideas that we have shared with students and many educators throughout the years.

Our intent is for you to take our ideas that work best with your particular students and modify as you see fit for your classroom.

Teaching Elementary School Students About the Brain: Using a Hand Model to Illustrate Three Parts of the Brain

Donna had an opportunity to teach students about their amazing brains at The Out-of-Door Academy in Sarasota, Florida. The purpose of the visit was for Donna and Marcus to produce a five-video companion streaming video series, *Teaching Students to Drive Their Brains,* as a companion to their 2016 book of the same name. The following excerpt from the first video could be adapted for teachers to use in their classrooms.

> Donna: Today we are going to learn about our amazing brain plasticity—our capacity to learn important knowledge and skills, while developing a growth mindset for learning. As we learn about our brains today, I'd like you to remember that each of you has an amazing, unique brain and that through practice and with the help of your teachers, every one of you will learn and remember a lot from school.
>
> [Donna points to the board.]
>
> Donna: On the board, I have written a thinking stem. Can anyone tell me what this thinking stem says?
>
> Student 1: My brain is brilliant because . . .
>
> Donna: Correct. My brain is brilliant because it can make a lot of connections. My brain is brilliant because I'm very curious about a lot of things. My brain is brilliant because I read a lot. My brain is brilliant because I love to learn and keep learning. Those are some of my personal reasons my brain is brilliant. All brains are different.
>
> Student 2: My brain is brilliant because I play the violin, I can do my homework, and I can run.
>
> Student 3: My brain is brilliant because I love to read and dance.
>
> [Before the end of the class discussion, all students have expressed how their brains are brilliant!]

Donna: Indeed, every brain is as unique as a fingerprint! Now that we all understand this, we are going to learn a model of three brain areas that each of us use each day. After we leave class, you can show this to your friends and your family. You can teach them about this brain model that has three parts (see Figure 2.1). So, to make our model brain, take your hand and make a fist. The space where your fingernails are down from your knuckles is the person's face, and the back of the head is on the other side of your knuckles down the back of your hand. The surface on the top of the skin of your fist represents the brain's *cortex*. Next, put your thumb inside your fist like this. Your thumb represents the *limbic system*. And, your wrist is where the *brain stem* is located. Below the brain stem is the spinal cord.

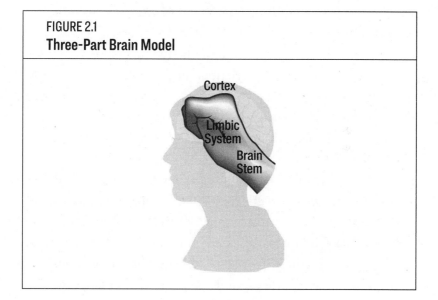

FIGURE 2.1
Three-Part Brain Model

Supporting Lesson on Basic Brain Structure and Functions

A brief lesson on the inner workings of the brain can support students' understanding that they are full of potential and that they can learn to become the "boss of their brains" (ASCD, 2018;

Conyers & Wilson, 2015a; Wilson & Conyers, 2014a, 2016a, 2020). The information that follows expands on the hand model lesson with descriptions of the brain's three major regions: the cerebral cortex, which controls higher-level functioning such as thinking, learning, understanding, and producing language; the limbic system, which controls the key functions of emotions and memory; and the brain stem, which connects the brain to the spinal cord and controls basic bodily functions. Let's look at each of these regions a little more closely.

Cerebral cortex and hemispheres. The *cerebral cortex* (also known as the *cortex* or *neocortex*), the outer layer of the cerebrum, is composed of gray matter folded in a labyrinth style that gives it a cauliflower-like appearance. Fotuhi describes the cortex as "ground zero" for "perceptual awareness, thought, language, and the ability to make decisions" (2013, p. 15).

The brain is divided into left and right hemispheres, which reflects the symmetry of the human body—that is, two eyes, two ears, two arms, two legs. The right hemisphere controls the motor functions on the left side of the body, whereas the left hemisphere controls the right side of the body.

While the hemispheres essentially mirror each other, each hemisphere also has its own specialty. For most people, the left hemisphere controls such abilities as language, math, and logic processing, while the right hemisphere supports spatial abilities, facial recognition, and other interpretive abilities. But even though some thinking abilities are more dominant in one hemisphere than the other, the two work together on most complex cognitive processes. One example is in the area of language. The left hemisphere does its part by deciphering sounds and determining syntax, while the right hemisphere contributes via understanding of the nuance of language as conveyed by such factors as rhythm and intonation (Tokuma-Espinosa, 2018; Zimmer, 2014).

Scientific evidence shows the adaptability of the brain and proves how extensive brain plasticity can be. Among the most remarkable and most-studied cases are those involving hemispheric division. In these cases, neurologists disconnected the brain hemispheres to eliminate debilitating seizures in patients who have had severe epilepsy. With extensive support and therapy, these patients were able to "retrain" their brains to varying degrees, so that some of the functions previously handled by one hemisphere could be taken over by the other hemisphere. The fact that the brain can so extensively rewire itself demonstrates that the brain is much more malleable than scientists once thought.

Limbic system. Another region of the brain that plays an important role in how we interact with the world around us is the *limbic system*. Located directly under the cortex, the limbic system is a group of interconnected structures in the frontal and temporal lobes and deeper parts of the brain. It is associated with regulating emotional activity, arousal/stimulation, and memory. Whereas the cortex can be termed metaphorically as the "thinking brain," the limbic system is more accurately characterized as the "feeling and reacting brain."

Within the limbic system is a pathway termed the "reward circuit," consisting of various linked brain structures that enable us to feel pleasure. Such feelings occur during learning as a result of the production of the neurotransmitter dopamine, which is triggered in response to rewarding experiences—for example, in achieving a goal. When we feel pleasure during learning, we are apt to be motivated to repeat behaviors. Dopamine is involved in many brain functions and plays an important role in many aspects of learning, including motivation, memory, and attention. The latter two aid in sustaining motivation to learn over time, since attention and memory help to ensure learning success.

The limbic system provides us with the important function of memory, with the hippocampus playing a key role. Fotuhi describes the hippocampus as "the gateway for new memories and essential for learning [as] the most malleable of [the] brain's regions" (2013, p. 16). The hippocampus receives input from throughout the neocortex and limbic system in serving its role in forming, storing, and processing memory.

Brain stem. The third major region of the brain is the *brain stem,* which connects the brain to the spinal cord. The brain stem, responsible for regulating heart and respiratory functions, plays a pivotal role in regulating sleep and consciousness cycles. Groups of cells in the brain stem connect directly with groups of cells elsewhere in the brain, meaning that the brain stem can influence responses to the neurons that conduct incoming stimuli throughout the midbrain and cortex, where higher levels of processing occur.

New imaging technologies have been useful in pinpointing the functions of these various structures in our brain and helping us to further understand the brain's plasticity. We have found that teachers and students alike are curious about the brain's plasticity and how our human brains are amazing in so many ways.

Extender

To see Donna modeling an example of how to teach students about their amazing and unique brains, visit http://www.ascd.org/professional-development/videos/teaching-students-to-drive-their-brains-videos.aspx. For additional information on this topic, check out a short YouTube video by Daniel Siegel (2016), clinical professor of psychiatry at the David Geffen School of Medicine at UCLA, who utilizes a similar model: https://www.youtube.com/watch?v=gm9CIJ74Oxw. In the video, Siegel explains to parents what is happening in their children's brains. To read about how to help parents support their children to understand their developing brains and use metacognition, see our article at https://www.parenttoolkit.com/social-and-emotional-development/news/self-awareness/how-to-help-your-child-understand-their-developing-brain.

We have taught educators to use and modify this lesson with students across a wide range of grade levels as part of the STEM curriculum and alongside other subjects. After sharing a similar lesson with her class, a K–5 teacher and instructional coach reveals that she led her class to create a character called Nancy Neuron to help the students understand how the brain changes during learning and to illustrate concepts of brain structure and functioning. She further stated that although her students can be hard to handle, this has "really transformed my classroom and helped them as individuals." After teaching students about their brilliant brains, teachers of young children may extend this lesson to help youngsters develop self-control, which is critical for regulating their emotions and behavior. We covered this topic in a blog post entitled, "Simple Ways to Help Young Kids Develop Self-Control" (Wilson & Conyers, 2016c), which can be found on the Edutopia website at https://www.edutopia.org/article/simple-ways-to-help-young-kids-develop-self-control-donna-wilson-marcus-conyers.

Middle School–High School: Changing Brains Through Learning and Growing Study Skills

Through the wonders of neuroplasticity, adolescents are ready and set to improve their performance in school and beyond. Adolescence is an exciting—albeit sometimes difficult—time as brains continue to develop and teenagers become increasingly independent, begin to look forward to life beyond high school, and go through many emotional, physical, and cognitive changes. The preteen and teenage years, beginning around age 12, are a period of astonishing changes in the brain. Educators can help teenagers learn how to take charge of their developing brains and steer their thinking in productive and positive directions toward success in college and in their lives and careers.

A Two-Part Lesson Framework

The following lesson framework can be useful as a means to (1) help students understand the power of their amazing brains and (2) learn about ways they can channel that power by using study strategies that can help them become more successful across learning contexts. This framework sets the stage for students to learn about what *neurons, cell bodies, axons, dendrites,* and *synapses* are and how they create connections that multiply in the brain when learning occurs.

This lesson provides the foundation for two crucial messages for middle and high school students to understand and internalize over time:

- *They have the capacity to change their brains and become functionally smarter.* This message is critically important because, unfortunately, many students are unaware of this fact. By the time students reach their early teens, they have formed an impression that they are either intellectually capable or not. Teachers should emphasize to students in the latter group that past school performance is not necessarily a predictor of future outcomes. They can change outcomes if they are willing to work hard when the learning gets challenging.
- *They can learn how to apply learning strategies, such as study skills, to become more successful learners.* Students who have not previously done well at school can learn effective study skills that will allow them to improve their grades and academic performance (Wilson & Conyers, 2016a, 2016b).

Part 1: Changing brains through learning. Holding up one hand with fingers spread out, the teacher explains that her fingers are the dendrites, her palm is the *cell body,* and her wrist and arm are the *axon* (see Figure 2.2). Holding up her second arm with her fingers almost touching the forearm of the first, she then explains that the gap between the *dendrites* (fingers) and axon (arm) is called the *synapse.*

Students can then share examples of knowledge or skills they have learned by creating new connections in their brains.

FIGURE 2.2
Representation of a Neural Connection

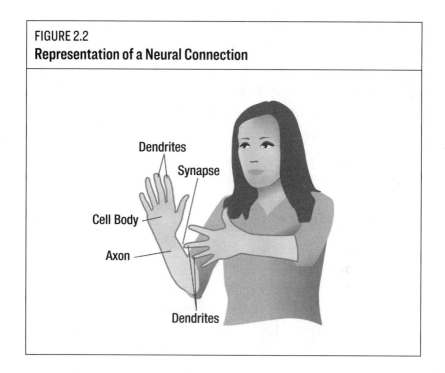

In another example of a way to drive home that students have the capacity to change their brains as they learn and to increase motivation to develop study skills, Michael Fitzgerald, an English teacher at Eagle Academy, an alternative high school for at-risk youth in Boise, Idaho, tells his students, "There are things in life you're not in charge of, but you are in charge of you." To illustrate what happens in students' brains when they learn, Mr. Fitzgerald draws a diagram of a *neuron* on the chalkboard and shows how synapses fire and form connections to other neurons in response to new experiences and learning (see Figure 2.3). He seeks to both empower students and challenge them to assume responsibility for their learning (Wilson & Conyers, 2016a).

Part 2: Sample study strategies. In the second part of this lesson framework, students learn a collection of sample study strategies to power their ability to learn, as they are expected to take on increasing responsibility for their learning in their middle school and high school years. These strategies enable students to become more independent and successful learners who can successfully complete both in-school and out-of-class assignments requiring independent research, reading for understanding, and wider application of classroom lessons.

FIGURE 2.3
Neurons Making Connections

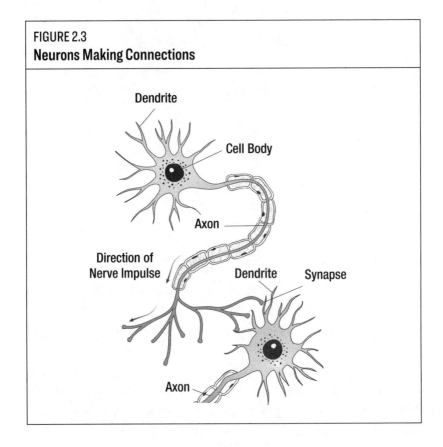

- *Make and adhere to a schedule.* Students can use the important executive functions of organizing and planning not only in school subjects but in their personal lives as well. Guide your students to develop a step-by-step process for their independent study projects, setting dates for the completion of each step. Suggest that they build in extra time for unexpected issues and remember to celebrate when steps are completed.

- *Read ahead to stay ahead.* Encourage students to finish their reading assignments by reading a few pages ahead. This strategy will help students improve their understanding and recall by showing them how the information presented in one chapter is applied and expanded on in the next.

- *Don't just read. Learn.* There is a big difference between reading words on the page and learning from them. To help students absorb the ideas from a reading assignment and improve recall of what they have read, suggest that they

—Create diagrams, pictures, and symbols to represent key ideas as they take notes.

—Summarize passages in their own words.

—Search for cues about the most important content. For textbook assignments, students can review key terms, subtitles, informational graphics, and other key features to reinforce crucial facts. When reading fiction or poetry, students should look for literary devices such as metaphors and symbols to uncover deeper meaning.

—Consistently test themselves on what they are reading so they can correct any misunderstandings and detect and remediate any gaps in their knowledge.

- *Consider the source.* A careful consideration of the credibility of sources that students consult and cite in their research projects, especially online sources, is a learning strategy that will serve them well throughout their academic lives and beyond. They should ask themselves such questions as, "Is the information I am reading or hearing fact or opinion? Is the objective of this resource to inform, to influence, or to entertain? Are the authors qualified to discuss the topic, and do the sources cited seem reputable?" These types of judgments represent a crucial executive function for students to develop. This careful approach to vetting information sources is one of the logical and predictive competencies that will support the resolution of academic and career challenges.

- *Create, then edit.* Students often get stymied at the beginning of an academic writing assignment because they are unsure of how to write a good introduction. One solution is to suggest students begin by writing down all the information they want to convey without worrying about how they will word the first paragraph. They may have an easier time writing the introduction once they have laid out all the content they have gathered. Another common problem among students is a failure to edit the first draft carefully. To help alleviate this problem, tell students to edit their papers not once but at least twice before turning in the assignment.

- *Identify which study skills work best for you.* Encourage students to try different strategies and stick with the ones that are most effective. For instance, some students may learn better by participating in study groups, while some may retain more by creating graphics to explore and connect the concepts they are studying. Still others may do best by reading and explaining the content aloud to themselves. The key is for students to be open to trying new strategies until they find one or two that give them the best results. Students' knowing the skills and strategies that work best for them is an aspect of metacognition—knowing yourself and knowing which tools can best help you accomplish tasks.

As your students explore these and other learning strategies we share throughout this book, remind them how changeable their brains are and how "practice makes cortex." Direct their thoughts and actions on learning new knowledge and skills, which will enable them to change their brains and become functionally smarter. Explain that if they are having difficulty with a particular subject, they can achieve the desired results through determination, hard work, and the use of several strategies until they hit on the ones that give them the best success, including asking for help when needed. Beyond this book, for more tools to teach students cognitive and metacognitive strategies that support the use of skills such as these, you might also want to check out our book, *Teaching Students to Drive Their Brains* (Wilson & Conyers, 2016a).

Selling Teens on the Power of Neuroplasticity and Their Potential to Learn at High Levels

A high school teacher and part-time coach who graduated from our program believes that the most important thing he can do for his students is to convince them that they can learn more than they think they can. His goal is to help students realize that they have the ability to succeed even if they have never excelled academically before. The biggest obstacle, this educator has found, is students' own preconceived notions that their intelligence is preset and they have no chance to improve. He strives to break down that preconception and give his students the confidence to realize that they can learn. To help them develop this confidence in their learning, he explains to his students that intelligence is not a fixed asset but can be enhanced through hard work and determination.

In this teacher's classroom, the focus is on helping students get out of a fixed mindset, in which they believe they are stuck where they are when it comes to learning. Some of these students are lagging behind in reading skills, but the teacher stresses that they can learn to read at a higher level. He wants them to realize that they can get better at reading and other skills, and he teaches strategies such as how to make inferences, predictions, and comparisons to help them achieve gains in reading.

To help the students understand their potential, the teacher describes the concept of neuroplasticity and the idea that our brains can change and that we can always get smarter. On the first day of class, he tells students: you're not just who you are today and hard work makes a difference. His philosophy of teaching is that nobody stays the same. A student will either get better or worse at learning. As educators, we must sell students on the idea that they can get better at learning and do what we can to help them move forward instead of backward by teaching them strategies for learning.

Extenders

For readers who are interested in learning more about the brain, you might want to check out a University of Washington resource for students and teachers alike: "Neuroscience for Kids," at http://faculty.washington.edu/chudler/dev.html. Another resource we recommend is *How We Learn: Why Brains Learn Better Than Any Machine...for Now* by cognitive neuroscientist Stanislas Dehaene (2020). His work connects well with the principles and practices we share in this book.

We also encourage interested teachers to participate in the Dana Foundation's Brain Awareness Week (http://www.dana.org/baw/about/). Our graduate Diane Dahl shares in her blog materials and activities she uses to teach students about their brilliant brains throughout the year, as well as examples of lessons she has created for Brain Awareness Week festivities (http://www.fortheloveofteaching.net/2012/03/brain-awareness-week-activities.html).

Supporting Positive Engagement and Energized Learning

When positive emotion energizes us, we are better able to concentrate, to figure out the social networks at a new job or new school, to broaden our thinking so we can creatively integrate diverse information, and to sustain our interest in a task so we can persevere.

—Richard Davidson, *The Emotional Life of Your Brain*
(2012, p. 89)

Principle 3: *Learn with practical optimism* as an approach to support a growth mindset through increased engagement, focused energy, and resilience in the face of challenges.

When we were developing the BrainSMART program, we asked teachers a key question: "What do you consider to be the most important factors in helping your students achieve greater academic success?" A common response was helping students maintain a state of positive engagement and optimism for learning so that they persist when the going gets tough. This response was consistent from elementary, middle, and high school teachers across all socioeconomic levels of student populations. Teachers emphasized how important it is to find ways to help students develop and sustain states of focused energy and greater engagement for learning over time. The consensus seemed to be that while many students have the capacity to learn well, they frequently lack the optimism, focus, and commitment to do the necessary work that would produce higher-level results. These views are reflected in students' responses to a Gallup poll of more than 700,000 5th through 12th graders: 29 percent indicated they are "not engaged," and 24 percent said they are "actively disengaged" in school (Gallup, 2017). In this chapter, we share research and methods for cultivating a classroom of students who exhibit *practical optimism*, sustain focused attention, and can engage positively in the process of learning.

Emotions: The Gateway to Learning

In 1994, Antonio Damasio published a groundbreaking work, *Descartes' Error: Emotion, Reason, and the Human Brain*, in which he delved extensively into the interconnectivity of brain and body functioning and emotions. Since then, others have added supportive research for the validity of this interdependence (e.g., Conyers & Wilson, 2015a, 2015b; Dehaene, 2020; Goleman, 2015; Immordino-Yang & Damasio, 2016; Immordino-Yang & Faeth, 2010; Ratey & Manning, 2015; van Geert & Steenbek, 2008). We use the term *body–brain system* to emphasize how the body, along with emotions and cognition, plays a role in influencing an individual's readiness, focus, motivation, and ability to learn (Wilson & Conyers, 2018). Through a combination of our physical, mental, and social-emotional systems, humans can achieve peak performance and a growth mindset for learning.

Damasio's more recent work, in concert with Immordino-Yang's, spotlights the importance of emotion in this equation. Specifically, "When educators fail to appreciate the importance of students' emotions, they fail to appreciate a critical force in students' learning. One could argue, in fact, that they fail to appreciate the very reason that students learn at all" (Immordino-Yang & Damasio, 2016, p. 40). Immordino-Yang and Damasio are among the researchers who support a contention that effective teachers have long known: the connection between learning and emotions is indisputable, and eliciting and sustaining a positive learning state in students is a prerequisite for boosting student achievement. Our BrainSMART approach (see the Appendix) encourages educators to create learning environments that put students in positive, low-stress, and high-challenge frames of mind.

Toward that end, we concur with research that advocates for *social and emotional learning,* defined as "the process of acquiring core competencies to recognize and manage emotions, set and achieve positive goals, appreciate the perspectives of others, establish and maintain positive relationships, make responsible decisions, and handle interpersonal situations constructively" (Durlak et al., 2011, p. 2). These are fundamental life skills that will serve students well throughout their personal, school, and work lives.

A 2011 meta-analysis by Joseph Durlak and colleagues found that students whose schooling incorporated instruction to develop competencies such as self-awareness, self-management, social awareness, relationship skills, and responsible decision making experienced significant academic gains—11 points higher than students who did not receive this type of instruction. The researchers attributed improved school outcomes to social and emotional learning that provides "a foundation for better adjust-ment and academic performance as reflected in more positive social behaviors, fewer conduct problems, less emotional distress, and improved test scores and grades" (p. 2). Many of the teaching strategies and techniques included in this chapter and throughout this book incorporate social and emotional learning components that, in turn, support developing and sustaining a growth mindset.

Practical Optimism at Work

Research finds that optimistic learners deal more effectively with stress and are more likely to carry on when encountering challenges (Davidson, 2012). Such learners persist, motivated by the belief that they can reach their learning goals. Researchers who have worked to coach students to become more optimistic about learning and more resilient when encountering challenges have found that "positive mood produces broader attention, more creative thinking, and more holistic thinking" (Seligman, 2011b, p. 80). Martin Seligman, a pioneer in the *positive psychology* move-ment, makes it clear that optimism is not a fixed attribute but rather is teachable and learnable: "We can teach our children the skills of a flexible and reality-based optimism" (1995, p. 9).

Teachers play an important role in guiding students to develop a growth mindset. By systematically modeling and elicit-ing healthy and optimistic states in their classrooms, teachers can boost student motivation for learning. In this chapter, we discuss research on the importance of the emotional state of students and their teachers and share strategies for encouraging positive learn-ing states in the classroom.

We use the term *practical optimism* to define an approach to learning and life that focuses on taking practical positive action and supporting positive learning states to increase the probabil-ity of successful outcomes (Wilson & Conyers, 2016a). Positive beliefs alone are not sufficient for success. As the definition suggests—and in line with Dweck's conceptualization of growth mindsets—taking action is an essential component in bearing out and actualizing those beliefs.

Positive Psychology

One way educators can support students in developing growth mindsets is by using key concepts from *positive psychology* to assist students in attaining higher levels of engagement, a more optimistic attitude, and greater motivation to learn. Positive psychology is defined as "the scientific study of the strengths that enable individuals and communities to thrive" (Positive Psychology Center, 2019). (To learn more about positive psychology, visit the Positive Psychology Center (https://ppc.sas.upenn.edu).)

Seligman, in *Learned Optimism* (2006), makes the case that educators, parents, and other caring adults must proactively teach children the tools they need to persist optimistically, which will increase the likelihood that they will succeed rather than giving in to failure and frustration. When students do not succeed immediately at a learning task, Seligman recommends these three questions (the three Ps) to assess their level of pessimism versus optimism:

- Is it personal?
- Is it permanent?
- Is it pervasive?

If students perceive that their lack of ability led to their academic failure, they are more likely to consider their deficiencies to be permanent and, consequently, develop a pessimistic outlook about their likelihood of success at learning tasks. By teaching students that failure is a temporary setback that can be overcome by using effective strategies, teachers help students build the sense of mastery that drives optimism, self-efficacy, and a growth mindset.

This is consistent with the BrainSMART principle: Never question ability; always improve strategy.

Self-Talk

Our inner thoughts and feelings impact how we feel and how well we relate to others. This provides good reason for educators to focus on helping students develop positive self-talk and a positive self-image that will extend outward. In our live workshops, we facilitate work in pairs to think about what Seligman's three questions might mean for student self-talk. Consider these two examples of the self-talk of two high school boys and the application of Seligman's three questions (see Figure 3.1).

Bill: I started this assignment on time but will never get it finished! It's too much work, and besides, I couldn't do it right anyway. I don't understand the subject, and why should I even try when the teacher can't explain it so I can understand? I got a bad grade on the last assignment, and I'll probably do worse on this one. Ugh! World history! Why do we have to study subjects like this? It doesn't matter. I'll never get into a good college anyway. The ACT is coming up, and I know I'm going to do terribly. These tests are so dumb. What's the point in even trying?

Jim: Glad I started this assignment early. I figured I might run into a couple snags. It is a little harder than I expected, but that extra reading sure did help. I wasn't super happy with my grade the last time, but the teacher gave me some really helpful feedback. So maybe I can boost that B to an A. Good thing I like history. It's cool to learn more about the world around us. If I can get this done tonight, I'll have the weekend to work on another ACT practice test. I'm glad I decided to take that prep course. Now I feel a lot less nervous about the ACT.

The differing perspectives of Bill and Jim are likely to correspond with different learning outcomes. Each student is in charge of how he views the assignment, and his thoughts have a big impact on his feelings and perceptions about the task and the consequences that are likely to result in terms of this assignment and his school and career trajectory. Modeling positive self-talk and reminding students about their amazing learning potential, giving feedback based on effort rather than ability, and teaching them learning strategies can help students like Bill begin to believe in themselves over time as they tackle learning challenges.

FIGURE 3.1
Applying Seligman's 3 *P*s to Student Self-Talk

Question that relates to outlook	Translation	Answer from Bill's point of view	How Jim might respond
Is it personal?	Is it really up to me?	I started this assignment on time but will never get it finished! I don't understand the subject because the teacher can't explain it so I can understand, and I got a bad grade last time.	I started the assignment early. It's harder than I thought, but that extra reading time really helped.
Is it permanent?	Will it be here forever? Can it be changed?	I'll never get into a good college anyway. What's the point in even trying?	If I can complete this assignment, I'll have time to study for the ACT. I took a prep course, which helped me feel less nervous about the ACT.
Is it pervasive?	Does it affect every part of my life?	Who needs to know about history and these other subjects anyway? The ACT is coming up, and I know I'm going to do terribly. These tests are so dumb.	The teacher gave me good feedback. I should be able to boost that B to an A. I like history. It's cool to learn about the world around us.

Practical Optimism Helps Students Develop Resilience

Sometimes school can be difficult for even the best learners. *Resilience* is a quality that allows some students to experience learning difficulties, be set back, and come back at least as strong as they were before. Instead of letting mistakes or other challenges overwhelm them, resilient people find ways to get up and move forward. David Yeager and Dweck (2012) found that when confronted with challenges such as bullying and underachievement, students who have had the opportunity to develop growth mindsets are more able to develop the resilience needed to overcome the trials and tribulations that sometimes come their way at school.

Optimism and a positive social-emotional outlook are among the factors that make students resilient and able to put forth continued effort to do or achieve their learning goals despite difficulties and setbacks. Optimism also helps lessen the effect of stress on the mind and body in the face of challenges. Using the strategies in this chapter that assist students to become more practically optimistic will also help them become more resilient.

Practical Optimism in the Face of Challenges

A Georgia elementary school teacher who studied with us shares an example of a student who was motivated to persist when confronted with difficulties. The student with failing test scores and a challenge with his speech had transferred from another school. Though enrolled in speech and language therapy, he never participated in class. The teacher recognized that the boy needed encouragement, so she told him, "Whatever you did before you got here doesn't matter. What you do from here on out is what determines my perception of you." With his teacher's support and encouragement, the boy became a student leader. After just nine weeks in the new class, he was able to improve his grades in every subject by 15 to 20 points. The boy's mother came to the first parent–teacher conference expecting to hear negative reports as she had in the past. Instead, she heard praise. The fact that someone saw promise in her son brought her to tears. "This student has opened up and leads discussions," the teacher reported. "I'm beginning to see him flourish. He goes home and completes all of his homework. I'm so proud of him" (Wilson & Conyers, 2013a, p. 14).

Approaching challenging learning situations with optimism increases the likelihood that students will persist and put in the hard work required to achieve success (Boman, Furlong, Shochet, Lilles, & Jones, 2009). They may encounter setbacks and disappointments along the way, but maintaining a growth mindset about optimism can help them surmount them. Physical activity is important as well, as it is known to boost mood and support a positive outlook that aids in achieving learning gains.

Maintaining an optimistic, upbeat outlook is helpful outside as well as inside of school. Davidson (2012) describes the various connections between how we feel and how well we think: when positive emotion empowers us, we achieve better focus, expand our thinking to become better problem solvers, enhance our creativity, and sustain interest in learning tasks in a way that allows us to persevere.

Psychologist Barbara Fredrickson also identified a connection between thoughts and emotions. In her book *Positivity* (2009), Fredrickson lays out her broaden-and-build theory, which posits that when we feel good about something, we tend to broaden our ideas about possible actions and become more aware of a wider range of possible thoughts and actions. Our graduate Kelly Rose, an instructional media specialist in Florida, illustrates the importance of practical optimism as an educator:

> Without it, my students would not be who they are. Practical optimism is why they are willing to design and code in a program that I do not even have experience with. It is why they are willing to try reading a book from a new genre, and why they are willing and able to be part of student-driven inquiry. It's why they are eager to learn anything new. I model this when working with my students as well as my

colleagues. It is important to me that everyone I work with celebrates success, but more important, that they also recognize opportunities for growth. There are far too many wonderful experiences in life. Without practical optimism, you are destined to miss out on those amazing opportunities. (Personal correspondence, April 9, 2019)

Modeling Positive Learning States

When educators model a positive, engaged state for teaching and learning, students are likely to become engaged in learning. Effective teachers have told us that when they are enthusiastic and engaged with students, their students respond in kind, participating in learning activities with excitement and engaging in interesting classroom discussions. Lessons seemed to fly by quickly, and occasionally there may have even been a few groans of disappointment when the class ended. These teachers and their students were experiencing *flow*, as described by Mihaly Csikszentmihalyi (2008). Csikszentmihalyi's flow theory describes an optimal psychological state that people experience when they are engaged in an activity that is interesting, engaging, and appropriately challenging for them. Flow often occurs when immersion in tasks and activities results in deep learning and high levels of satisfaction.

When educators model positive learning states, they are supporting students' engagement in learning. It is not superfluous. Rather it is a foundation of effective teaching and learning. When students are positively engaged and focused on learning, they experience more growth and are more likely to develop a growth mindset. You can model positively engaged states for learning by

- Sharing what you are excited about learning and telling your students why you are keen to learn it.
- Discussing your love of reading and how what you have read has made a positive difference in your life.
- Sharing how learning has changed your life for the better.

Five Strategies for Developing Students' Practical Optimism

To develop students' practical optimism

- *At the end of a class period, advisory, or school day, ask students to recall one thing that has gone well for them.* We have found that some students who have learning challenges need assistance to come up with even one item, especially when this strategy is first used.
- *At the beginning of the school day, encourage students to reflect on a positive experience they had the day before.* This can help even struggling students begin their day on a more upbeat note.
- *Nurture students to keep a daily record of their incremental progress using different modalities* such as a picture, journal entry, or brief and informal video.
- *Support students in identifying and expressing feelings of gratitude.* Send students on a hunt at the beginning of the week to capture moments for which they are thankful by taking a photo or jotting down notes. At the end of the week, invite students to share examples of people and experiences for which they feel grateful.
- *Encourage students to look forward to new learning experiences with anticipation and excitement rather than fear.* As you assist students in becoming more optimistic, they will be better equipped to learn the skills needed to achieve their goals and make the most of opportunities as they arise—in other words, to exhibit a growth mindset!

Extender

Many educators have shared that parents are keen to learn how to assist their children to become more optimistic about learning. The five strategies can be shared with parents to adapt for use at home. Over the years, we have heard from teachers who have supported their own children to become ever more optimistic, and they, too, have further developed this essential capability.

Learning to Deal with Stress

Everyone deals with stress at some point in their lives, but it can have a debilitating impact on the learning of students who become overly anxious when they are called on to answer a question, take a test, or stand before a class to make a presentation. For children who experience chronic stress as a result of their home environments, school can be like an oasis in the desert.

There is a physiological reason that stress makes learning more difficult. During high-stress situations, the blood is moving away from the cortical areas of the brain, where complex thought occurs, into the survival areas of the brain, which are involved in the fight-or-flight response. As a result, a student's cognitive processing system is generally less effective. Optimal learning is more likely to occur when the student can move beyond the mere absence of threat to learn in a positive school and classroom environment.

Thoughtful and caring educators can be effective allies in helping students overcome harmful stress. Among the strategies they can use is talking with students about the signs of academic stress and showing them how to use self-regulation techniques to overcome it. Cecelia Beagle, a middle school English and language arts teacher, has used both of those strategies successfully (Wilson & Conyers, 2014a). She begins by talking with her students about how stressing out before or during a test can make it harder to think clearly and remember what they've learned. When students confirm that they often feel nervous before taking a big test, Ms. Beagle asks them what impact they think that stress will have on their ability to do well. The students share responses that can best be summarized by this one: "I studied really hard, but when I looked at the test, it was like my mind went blank."

Ms. Beagle assures her students that it's possible to overcome the negative aspects of stress. She shows them how to recognize the signs of stress and discusses the importance of taking steps to relax and get in a more positive state for learning prior to taking a test. Then she leads them in an exercise and stretching regimen to turn their stress into positive energy. With techniques such as these, students are able to become more relaxed and ready to focus on the test. Over time, this stress-reduction strategy has become a routine before tests in Ms. Beagle's classroom, progressing to the point that students began volunteering to lead the class in the stretching exercises. She reports a "remarkable difference in the confidence and energy that flows in my classroom while the students are testing." These strategies have had a positive impact on students in improving their learning readiness and equipping them with useful strategies for high school, college, and beyond.

Four Strategies for Helping High Schoolers Deal with Stress

Academic stress may be even worse in high school students, who are feeling the pressure to get good grades in the lead-up to college. Educators can help these students overcome academic stress in the following ways:

- Help students understand the reasons behind their varying emotions and mood swings by teaching them about the changes that are occurring in the brain.
- Provide students with opportunities to share their thoughts and feelings. Ask open-ended questions such as, "How does that make you feel?" and "What would make things better?"
- Use role-playing to help students learn how to deal with potentially difficult situations. At first, you may find that they need some assistance to identify situations that might possibly be tricky.

- Talk to students about age-appropriate, healthy ways to deal with stress. Among the strategies that might prove most effective are physical exercise, journaling, peer support groups, yoga, tai chi, and meditation.

The best ways to help students move beyond feeling threatened and anxious are to guide them in developing a practical optimistic outlook and to use methods discussed in Chapter 4, such as praising students for both accomplishment and effort, giving learners choices, and increasing internal motivation. Choice, control, and experiences of success foster internal motivation and create engaged learners who are apt to have growth mindsets (National Academies of Sciences, Engineering, and Medicine, 2018).

Teacher-Tested Techniques: Recognizing and Managing Emotions

A fundamental aspect of school-based programs to promote social and emotional learning "involves instruction in processing, integrating, and selectively applying social and emotional skills in developmentally, contextually, and culturally appropriate ways" (Durlak et al., 2011, p. 3). This focus reflects the benefits of guiding students in maintaining a growth mindset and practical optimism in their academic pursuits. The following techniques offer a framework for discussing how taking charge of one's emotions can support more productive learning and for guiding students to recognize and deal with negative emotions that threaten to derail learning and interactions with their peers.

Discussion on Controlling Emotions for Positive Learning Outcomes

A crucial aspect of metacognition is self-awareness (see Chapter 1), and an important aspect of self-awareness is being conscious of our emotions during learning. Educators can help students understand how their emotions play a role in aiding them in becoming more successful at learning (see Figure 3.2). Lead a discussion with students to identify things they can focus on in the daily school environment, placing them along a continuum that ranges from Relaxed Positive (having fun with friends) and Useful Positive (engaged in learning) to Useless Negative (dwelling on thoughts that serve little purpose other than to make them feel bad). In the middle of this continuum are neutral activities that have little emotional impact, and what we refer to as Useful Negatives are activities and tasks that may seem irritating and frustrating but ultimately lead to learning progress and thus a path to more positive states (Conyers & Wilson, 2015a).

FIGURE 3.2
Continuum of Emotions in Daily Life

Relaxed Positive	Enjoying lunch, socializing with friends, playing music, recess
Useful Positive	Working on a project of your choice, practicing a sport, learning a new language
Useful Neutral	Completing a set of math problems, reading an assignment for class
Useful Negative	Feeling overwhelmed at the beginning of a project but staying resolved to develop a plan and learn the necessary skills to tackle it; practicing until the skills are learned
Useless Negative	Blaming, complaining, whining about perceived slights by others

Helping Students Cope with Negative Emotions

While emphasizing that positivity can help support learning gains, educators should let students know that both positive and negative emotions are natural and that a wide range of emotions is to be expected throughout life. To assist students with their emotional lives in a way that will positively impact their learning, educators can

- *Encourage conversations about emotional responses in discussions about stories and books, history lessons, and classroom situations* (e.g., "How do you think this character felt in this situation? Angry? Worried? Scared?" or "The people who were part of the Underground Railroad took big risks to help others escape slavery. Can you imagine how they coped with their fears and worries?").
- *Give students a chance to express their emotions, both positive and negative.* Acknowledge and express empathy in one-on-one conversations rather than ignoring negative emotions (e.g., "I could be wrong, but you seem sad about what happened on the playground. I would be sad if that happened to me too" or "It seems like you are feeling frustrated right now. Do you want to talk about that?"). It may be helpful to suggest some coping strategies, such as taking a deep breath in and out or thinking a calming thought ("It's OK. I can get through this"), but don't gloss over their feelings.
- *Step in when negative emotions arise in a classroom setting to emphasize that learning can be hard work—with a positive payoff if they persist and ask for help when needed.* Help students understand that negative emotions such as doubt, confusion, and frustration are not all bad. They can provide the motivation to grow. Look for opportunities to acknowledge when students work through their tough feelings ("I know that some of you are nervous about making a presentation in front of the class, but you did a great job!").

Extender

If you are an educator who wants to go beyond the classroom to facilitate an optimistic and growth-minded school culture, consider reading our *edCircuit* article (Conyers & Wilson, n.d.) at https://www.edcircuit.com/effects-positive-mindset-school-culture/. In this piece, we share how teachers, teacher leaders, and administrators alike can lead toward greater positivity and well-being within our schools.

Physical Activity Helps Create Focused Attention and Energized Learning

Learning requires a great deal of focused energy. One of the best ways to help boost students' energy and attention—and support a more positive social-emotional outlook—is to incorporate movement and exercise into the school day. A 2010 report from the Centers for Disease Control and Prevention—summarizing 50 studies involving physical activity breaks in the classroom, physical education, after-school sports and other activities, and active play during recess—found positive associations with academic performance. At the same time, this meta-analysis found no negative outcomes for making physical activity a regular part of the school day. This important finding should alleviate concerns that taking time away from core subjects for movement and play might decrease test scores and grades (Conyers & Wilson, 2015b).

Exercise fuels positive mood through the release of neurochemicals such as endorphins, serotonin, and melatonin. Neurochemicals increase neural activation in the parts of the brain associated with positive emotions, and they also increase focus and attention (Hecht, 2013). Because of the near-instantaneous impact that exercise has in boosting mood, it has been shown to be effective in alleviating anxiety and depression (Weir, 2011). Moreover, it is an effective antidote to unhealthy stress that can impact learning.

Another positive impact of exercise is that it may have both a physiological and developmental impact on children's brains. Among the physical manifestations that can occur are increased oxygen to the brain that may enhance learning, alterations to neurotransmitters, and structural changes in the central nervous system (Wilson & Conyers, 2014b). Regular physical activity increases the production of brain chemicals and supports the production of new neurons and synapses.

In addition, regular physical activity completes a positive feedback loop supporting learning and a growth mindset. The relationship between physical activity and optimism may convey several benefits that extend to facilitating academic performance. Students experience a boost in mood after exercising, and their feelings of self-efficacy and mastery in completing the physical activity further reinforce a positive, can-do attitude. In short, regular exercise boosts both cognitive functioning and an optimistic outlook (Conyers & Wilson, 2015b, para. 16).

Five Strategies for Incorporating Movement into Learning

To incorporate movement into learning

- *Get students moving at various times during the school day.* Encourage students to be physically active during the course of their day, such as on their way to and from school, at recess, during P.E. class, between classes, and even as part of classroom lessons. In fact, incorporating movement into lessons—in the form of an active game, for instance—is a way to reinforce content while also providing the added benefit of making learning fun, engaging, and memorable.

- *Give students time to engage in some form of physical activity immediately before academically challenging coursework and tests.* An excellent example comes from Naperville (Illinois) High School, where students who took a physical education class, appropriately titled "Learning Readiness P.E.," right before a literacy class improved their literacy skills by twice as much as students who had several hours between physical education and the literacy class (Conyers & Wilson, 2015b).

- *Start the day with movement.* Some of the most effective teachers help students get energized for the school day ahead with a variety of exercises such as stretches, jumping jacks, and arm crosses. To incorporate this idea for the entire school, administrators and teachers may wish to consider leading a morning warm-up routine that is broadcast to classrooms over closed-circuit TV or the loudspeaker (Wilson & Conyers, 2014b).
- *Get creative!* We can cite several examples of educators who are using innovative strategies to incorporate movement into learning activities. Kelly Rose, mentioned earlier in this chapter, employs "brains breaks" at her primary school as a way to incorporate movement into library activities. Another activity she has used is to share a dance video during a school assembly that gets the entire school up and moving. Realizing that students sometimes have a hard time just sitting at their desks, Georgia middle school teacher Maureen Ryan keeps a stationary bike in her health classroom as a way to encourage students to take turns pedaling and reading without disrupting the instructional flow.
- *Emphasize the role of exercise in learning success.* Helping students understand that physical activity makes their brains function more effectively and efficiently gives them one more reason to make exercise a lifelong habit. If you are able to help students make physical activity a part of their everyday lives, not only will that serve them well in school, it will also help them in their personal lives and future careers.

Teacher-Tested Techniques: Fostering Positive Engagement in Learning

When students are in a positive social-emotional state and engaged in learning tasks, their brains operate at a peak level—

fully focused, on the ball, alert, and creating positive changes in their brains (Merzenich, 2013). Contrast this with students who are in a negative or bored state, in which various distractions may keep them from learning. For example, they might have a pessimistic attitude about learning, be concerned that they can't do the work, or lack energy or focus for learning. Teachers have told us that the following tools have helped them support their students' peak learning states.

High-Five, Step by Step

Students are better able to develop the habit of consistently focusing on what's useful and positive in their lives through the encouragement of teachers and parents. An effective way to enhance this focus is to use the high-five method (Wilson & Conyers, 2018, p. 243), which introduces the concept of positive learning. When using this strategy, ensure that all students have a chance to participate.

Step 1. Ask your students if they would like to learn a way to more consistently sustain positive learning states.

Step 2. After an age-appropriate discussion about the benefits of positive learning, read aloud the following story about treasure hunters and trash collectors.

Treasure Hunters and Trash Collectors

It seems that, in life, there are two types of people. The first are treasure hunters. Every day they seek out what is useful and positive. They focus on it, talk about it, and think about it. Each of these moments is treasured like a bright, shining jewel that they store in their treasure chest forever.

And then there are trash collectors, who spend their lives looking for what is wrong, unfair, and not working. They focus their energy, time, and thoughts on trash, and every day they put that trash into a big trash can.

Every day the treasure hunters proudly carry their treasure into the future, while the trash collectors drag their heavy, smelly trash can from one day to the next. The question is: "When they get to the end of the year, what does each person have—a treasure chest filled with useful, positive memories, or a trash can full of things they didn't like?"

The choice is yours. You get to decide.

Step 3. Ask your students if they would like a simple way to become more of a treasure hunter.

Step 4. Ask students to think of five things that they could feel good about—five things in their lives that they like.

Step 5. Ask your students to draw a mind map or write or draw about their five things.

Step 6. Tell students to go to five other people, give them a high-five, and read to them their list of five things.

Step 7. Continue using this process once a week or once a month and encourage students to find more and new things to put on their high-five lists.

This simple technique is a wonderful way to get students to begin to focus on what's useful and positive. The power of this technique is enhanced when teachers model it on a monthly, weekly, or even daily basis and link it to growth mindsets when most appropriate.

Ball Toss, Step by Step

The Ball Toss (Wilson & Conyers, 2018, p. 229) can be used to help students get reenergized and refocused on positive learning.

Step 1. Present information to your students in a positive and powerful way.

Step 2. Ensure that there is a good level of retention and recall of the material by asking questions and asking students to create a mind map or other graphic organizer.

Step 3. After you feel there is an adequate level of knowledge, begin the ball toss-game.

Step 4. Direct students to pass the ball to one another. Whenever a student picks up the ball, she says just one thing she knows about the topic. After a student catches the ball and shares one fact, he throws the ball to another person, who has to say something else about the topic.

Step 5. At the end of the exercise, congratulate everybody on their focus and prepare for the next stage of learning.

This exercise can help get students back into a focused and positive learning state. It allows them to demonstrate what they know and also get some practice at remembering information under stress.

Motivating Growth Mindsets Through Goals and Feedback

Motivation is distinguishable from general cognitive functioning and helps to explain gains in achievement independent of scores on intelligence tests.

—National Academies of Sciences, Engineering, and Medicine,
How People Learn II: Learners, Contexts, and Cultures
(2018, p. 109)

Principle 4: *Set growth goals* and establish targets with a level of challenge that is not too easy or too difficult.

We are inspired by visits to classrooms where teachers have created conditions for increasing student motivation. They have done so by applying ideas we are sharing in this chapter. Donna wishes she had been equipped with this understanding when she was studying to become a teacher. However, she had little in the way of knowledge or methods to prepare her to help children who came to school without the motivation to learn. Armed with strategies that were just a step or two beyond bribing children with candy, she was in serious need of a usable understanding of motivation in a 3rd grade classroom with around 30 students, two-thirds of whom were active boys and a good number with learning challenges. Fortunately, with the advent of the 1980s, the research base on motivation and learning grew rapidly. The work of researchers such as Bernard Weiner and Carol Dweck began to emerge and gain prominence. By the early 1990s, during her doctoral work at the University of Oklahoma, she had the opportunity to study the stream of research on motivation that continues today.

When Dweck was conducting research with students, a metaphorical lightbulb switched on for her when she found that some students grew more motivated and determined to learn in the face of challenge and failure. For example,

> Confronted with the hard puzzles, one 10-year-old boy pulled up his chair, rubbed his hands together, smacked his lips, and cried out, "I love a challenge!" Another, sweating away on these puzzles, looked up with a pleased expression and said with authority, "You know, I was *hoping* this would be informative!" (Dweck, 2016a, p. 3)

In essence, some students in Dweck's study were exhibiting a growth mindset. They were positively engaged and motivated by taking on challenging goals and learning from failure and setbacks. This chapter focuses on key concepts for encouraging and sustaining higher levels of motivation while developing growth mindsets.

Motivation Matters

No matter how you define motivation, it has a clear impact on learning. Motivation is described as "a condition that activates and sustains behavior toward a goal. It is critical to learning and achievement across the lifespan" (National Academies of Sciences, Engineering, and Medicine, 2018). Motivation can occur in many different forms—from being inspired to create a set of broad goals or objectives to having the drive to accomplish a difficult task. Motivation is vital to students' success in school and in other aspects of their lives (Anderman & Sayers, 2020; Fredericks et al., 2011; Lazowski & Hulleman, 2016; National Academies of Sciences, Engineering, and Medicine, 2018; National Research Council and Institute of Medicine, 2004). Researchers have found that "when students are motivated, they learn more, persist longer, create higher-quality work, earn better grades, and score higher on standardized tests" (Hennessey, 2016, p. 1).

When Melissa Smith was teaching English as a second language to K–5 students in Grayson, Georgia, she found that a teacher's excitement about learning words in a new language can be contagious. She recalls the story of "Maria" to illustrate how that excitement can fuel learning motivation: Maria takes the initiative to share a new word with her teacher every morning during the school breakfast program. "She'll come up to me and say, 'Creation is a noun,' and we talk about parts of speech and suffixes," Ms. Smith says. "And then I might say, 'We're done with the -tions, a suffix usually found in a noun. Bring me some -ates. Those are usually verbs.' She came in one morning with differentiate, and I was astounded. She goes home every day and looks up a new word" (Wilson & Conyers, 2013a, p. 11). This story shows how getting students excited about a topic of study will make them more motivated to sustain active engagement in learning.

Maintaining high expectations for students also enhances their learning motivation. Educational researcher John Hattie highlights the importance of high expectations for each student who enters the classroom, stating that "our role is to create new horizons of success and then to help the students to obtain them" (2012, p. 83). Effective educators who embody a growth mindset convey the important message that all students can learn and succeed. The growth mindset teacher who has high expectations for all students and conveys the message that success is the result of the effort and strategies used each day is guiding students to reach more of their potential.

Educational philosopher Israel Scheffler emphasizes the critical importance of the educator's role in helping children achieve their potential:

> Children do not have any way of assessing their own powers at the onset. They learn what they can do by absorbing the beliefs of their elders as the confirmation of potential the child did not believe it had. Such mastery is facilitated by the teacher's display of faith in the student's potential, which overcomes the student's groundless skepticism. (2010, p. 66)

By "groundless skepticism," Scheffler is commenting on the notion that young people often underestimate the scope of what they can achieve. Therefore, more experienced, significant people in their lives, including their teachers and parents, must help them set their sights on challenging but achievable goals.

Assisting Students to Set High Expectations with Challenging, Achievable Goals

Benefits of Goal Setting

A valuable strategy that has been shown to increase motivation is goal setting (National Academies of Sciences, Engineering, and Medicine, 2018). Teaching students to set appropriate goals helps empower them to adopt a growth mindset, own their learning, and improve achievement. When students are taught how to set and achieve personal goals, they can choose what they want to think and learn about, improve, and achieve. The process of setting goals encourages them to determine a long-term vision of what they want to do and the short-term motivation to keep them energized so that they will work hard along the way.

Gary Latham (n.d.) outlined four main benefits of goal setting:

- It increases and focuses our attention on the project or activity at hand.
- It is energizing and increases our effort level.
- It helps us persist over time.
- It helps us create strategies and alternative routes to achievement.

Additionally, students who set their own personal learning goals said they experienced more positive moods than those who did not set personal goals, and they also experienced a greater sense of well-being (Morisano et al., 2010). This is an especially important finding for students with learning challenges, as confirmed by Heidi Grant and Dweck (2003), who found that learning goals have been shown to positively influence achievement despite setbacks and even poor self-efficacy.

There is significant research that confirms the correlation between student achievement and goal setting. One study shows that students who took part in a goal-setting program for struggling students increased their GPAs by 30 percent, while another found that students who have clear, specific, and challenging yet attainable goals are more likely to be successful in college (Morisano, Hirsh, Peterson, Phil, & Shore, 2010), most likely because the "goals direct a student's attention toward the goal, increase effort and persistence, and motivate a student to find strategies to attain the goal" (Latham, n.d., para. 1).

Learning Goals Are Key to Creating Growth Mindsets

An explicit link between goals and motivation is central to *achievement goal orientation theory* (Ames & Archer, 1988; Dweck & Leggett, 1988; Elliot & Hulleman, 2017), which describes how motivation for learning tasks varies based on one's goal orientation toward either mastery or performance goals. In the case of *mastery (learning) goal orientation*, people focus on building skills and increasing understanding. Their goals are long term and internally driven. An example of such a goal would be becoming fluent in Spanish. Studies show that people are more likely to persist and work hard when driven by learning goals—and more likely to enjoy the experience (Halvorson, 2012 ; Svinicki, 2016).

Conversely, in the case of a *performance goal orientation*, people tend to focus on external goals, such as how teachers, peers, and others will judge their work. These goals are usually short term and finite—for instance, getting an *A* on their next Spanish test rather than learning Spanish as a lifelong skill. Since those who have a performance goal orientation often tie success or failure to feelings of self-worth, encountering challenges when pursuing such goals can thwart motivation. Initial failure can lead to a loss of self-confidence and a tendency to give up. With this in mind, researchers have identified two subsets of performance goal orientation: performance approach orientation, in which people work hard to illustrate their competence and reinforce positive feelings about themselves, and performance avoidance orientation, in which people are reluctant to attempt a new skill because they are fearful of making mistakes or appearing incompetent (Elliot & Hulleman, 2017; Svinicki, 2016). Because students with this orientation are likely to shy away from academic risks, it's important to help them realize that making mistakes is not a source of embarrassment but rather an important part of learning.

Teachers who place a high value on learning or mastery goals are more likely to create a classroom that results in positive outcomes, characterized by a greater use of strategies to help students more effectively process information; a focus on persistence in the face of learning challenges; and a process for helping students achieve more sustained interest in learning (Latham, n.d.). It will likely be easier for teachers to help students establish realistic but challenging goals in classrooms that have a learning goal structure in place, rather than an overemphasis on performance through too much focus on testing and grades (National Academies of Sciences, Engineering, and Medicine, 2018).

Five Strategies for Setting and Reaching Growth Goals

Setting learning goals at an appropriate level of challenge is key to motivation and sustaining learning. Educators can help students courageously confront learning challenges by reminding them about their brains' amazing plasticity, which allows them to "rewire their brains" with each learning gain. In addition, students benefit when teachers provide additional support in the form of teaching and reinforcing the use of learning strategies that can help students set and progress toward their goals.

Student goals should be intrinsically motivating and doable but challenging. The following strategies can be helpful in guiding students to set their learning goals at what we call the Goldilocks level of challenge—not too difficult, not too easy, but just right:

- *Advise students to define their goals by identifying in clear terms what they hope to accomplish.* To increase motivation, give students choices in the content of their projects, materials, and activities when possible (see the following Teacher-Tested Technique). Assist students in putting their goals in writing and posting them where they will be able to see them each day.
- *Help students think through the process of accomplishing a goal* from start to finish with a measurable plan for success.
- *Remind students that big goals are achieved by planning and working through* a series of smaller, more manageable steps to keep making progress.
- *Begin new units and projects by having students fill in a graphic organizer* to identify what they will be studying, why it is important, and what steps are required to reach their goals.

- *Celebrate incremental wins.* As each small step is reached, suggest that students recognize their accomplishments and internalize their wins.

Teacher-Tested Technique: Increasing Motivation Through Choice

When teachers assist students in choosing their classroom goals, there is a much greater chance that students will be motivated to engage in the effort required in learning. Giving students choices is one of the most powerful ways teachers can increase student motivation (Anderson, 2016). Personal interest is an important area for Dweck and other mindset researchers, leading to numerous studies on implicit theories of interest, the idea that personal interests are somewhat fixed (fixed mindset) or that they can be developed (growth mindset). A significant finding from this research is that people who have a growth mindset find it easier to develop new interests (O'Keefe, Dweck, & Walton, 2018a, 2018b). This finding suggests that educators who want their students to develop and sustain new interests should guide them to develop a growth mindset.

Guiding students to set learning goals based on their personal interests is another important aspect of their self-awareness, a facet of metacognition (discussed in Chapter 1). For example, Donna had an opportunity to observe young students at Portfolio School in New York City, where the core mission of educators is to inspire students to develop the intrinsic motivation to learn. There she dialogued with passionate learners engaged in problem solving, innovating, and communicating to inspire as they participated in project-based learning.

Letting Learners Choose

To personalize instruction and enhance students' interest, motivation, and engagement, encourage them to select topics of personal interest to read, study, or pursue as the subject of a learning project. Giving students choices helps underscore that they are in charge of their learning, have control of their learning goals, and can work toward success through the use of strategies such as devoting an appropriate amount of time to an assignment.

To encourage high motivational levels through the use of student choice, teachers enjoy using or modifying the following aspects of choice strategy:

- For part of your teaching time, select a range of topics that are relevant to the curriculum.
- Offer choices to your students about what they study.
- When students finish a task early, suggest that they work on one of the topics.
- Set a period of time on which students can work on the topics throughout the year.
- Use students as topic experts.
- As a further boost to student achievement, give students a choice of how to demonstrate what they have learned, when appropriate. For example, let students choose from drawing, writing, speaking, or acting it out (Wilson & Conyers, 2018, p. 273).

Principle 5: *Get the feedback needed* to continuously improve learning and sustain a growth mindset.

Giving Students Feedback That Supports Motivation

Feedback on goal progress enables students to track how well they are advancing toward achieving their learning goals. By assisting students in understanding that the outcome can be changed for the better and that their poor performance is attributable to causes over which they have control, teachers can give students hope that they'll be able to succeed by working harder or trying a different strategy. Educators are in a unique position to boost student confidence by fostering the belief that intelligence and ability can be developed through employing greater effort and finding more effective strategies (American Psychological Association, 2015).

Helping Students Develop a Sense of Control Over Their Learning Outcomes

If you feel that you, rather than others, are the main driver of your success, you're more likely to have the motivation to work hard to achieve it. Bernard Weiner's (1992, 2018) *attribution theory* focuses on how people explain their own successes or failures, particularly in terms of achievement. Weiner's understanding of attribution encompasses three factors: *locus of control, stability,* and *controllability*. Understanding these factors can help us guide students toward a greater sense of control of their learning.

Locus of control. Whether the student believes success or failure is based on an internal cause (such as the amount of time she spent studying) or an external cause (such as the way in which the teacher graded or presented the material).

Students who believe they are responsible for their success are likely to feel a sense of accomplishment and confidence in their ability to learn. This is likely to fuel continued motivation and efforts to succeed. Conversely, if they attribute their success to someone else—"The teacher gave me an *A*"—they are less likely to feel the sense of pride and confidence that should result from the effort they exerted to excel academically.

When students perform poorly, they might reason that they received a poor grade on a test because the teacher did not adequately explain the material, disregarding the fact that they didn't study. Since they are not accepting responsibility for their poor performance, they are unlikely to learn from this outcome that they should study harder the next time. Rather, they may continue down the same path by blaming others and refusing to accept responsibility for their own mistakes.

Educators can assist students in developing an internal locus of control by asking guiding questions to help them focus on the process of learning, such as:

- When have you successfully finished a learning task before?
- What is the next goal you want to achieve?
- When have you shown an optimistic spirit to overcome a learning challenge?
- What are the key strategies you can use to give yourself the greatest chance of success?

Stability. Whether the student thinks the cause of success or failure is likely to remain the same every time or to vary and produce a different outcome next time.

How people attribute their successes or failures (their beliefs about why they succeeded or failed) influences the amount of effort they will put forth for the same activity the next time. Students are more likely to be motivated to put in the effort if they believe that they have control over an outcome and that the outcome can be changed. Educators can help students understand that they can change the outcome to a more successful one by giving feedback such as:

- Do you think your grade might be better the next time if you spend more time on the next project?
- You really stuck to that until you got it. That's wonderful!
- You have had difficulty with assignments like this one before. This was a hard project, but you completed it one step at a time and it turned out well!

Controllability. Whether the student thinks she can control the cause of the outcome. Controllable causes might be the amount of effort spent on homework, while an example of an uncontrollable cause is a belief that math ability is innate. In other words, students are less likely to apply effort if they believe they don't have the ability to succeed due to an uncontrollable cause.

To underscore that students control the causes of their learning outcomes, focus on their efforts and use of effective strategies when praising improvement. Be specific rather than vague. For example:

- You worked so hard on learning the new words in this story that you can read the whole book now. That's great!
- This project obviously took a lot of effort. Tell me about how you put it all together.
- Instead of just asking what it means, you looked up the word online yourself. That's wonderful!
- Looks like doing your math homework is paying off. You got an *A* on this week's quiz!
- Yes, you *can* do it! I am so proud to hear you say that.
- I like how you chose the harder problems today. You will learn some new things!

Praise and Mindsets

Claudia Mueller and Dweck have found that praising students for their ability (for example, telling them they are smart after scoring high on a test) reinforces a fixed mindset. Such praise has the unintended consequence of associating failure with lack of ability. As a result, students may then begin to fear failure and give up when the going gets tough. Conversely, praising students for their efforts or a strategy they used (as in the examples in the previous section) has been proven to help them develop a growth mindset and foster resilience to bounce back after difficulties (Mueller & Dweck, 1998). Making a connection between hard work and the ability to learn is imperative since "students who see the value of effort and hard work in achieving their goals are more likely to be motivated and to push themselves" (Sternberg & Williams, 2010, p. 377). Such motivation is inherent in those who want to achieve continuous development and improvement. Dweck sums it up: "For students with the growth mindset, it doesn't make sense to stop trying" (2016a, p. 59).

Two Different Mindsets

The matrix in Figure 4.1 provides an at-a-glance summary of the relationship of people's views regarding mindsets, functional intelligence, goal orientations, and attributions for outcomes, all facets of learning that are important for learning success across the lifespan and various contexts (Wilson & Conyers, 2020, p. 79).

FIGURE 4.1
Mindset Matrix

People who have a fixed mindset...	People who have a growth mindset...
Believe that intellectual abilities are static and largely unchangeable.	Believe that intellectual abilities are malleable and can be improved through learning, repetition, and hard work.
Have a performance goal orientation.	Have a mastery (learning) goal orientation.
Attribute their successes and failures to external, stable, and uncontrollable causes.	Attribute their successes and failures to internal, unstable, and controllable causes.

The Importance of Grit and How to Help Students Develop It

Learning anything at some point may get difficult. People with a growth mindset persist in the face of difficulty by trying different strategies—investing more time and practice or asking for more help, for example. Applying persistence in the face of challenges has come to be known as *grit*, defined as the perseverance and passion to achieve long-term goals. Grit has been found to be an important factor for achieving success across academic and career contexts (Duckworth, Peterson, Matthews, & Kelly,

2007; Duckworth et al., 2019). These findings suggest that the achievement of challenging goals entails not only ability but also the persistent application of ability over the course of time.

As teachers help students develop a growth mindset, they are also helping them develop a capacity for grit. If students believe they can become functionally smarter, it makes sense to keep trying even when the task is difficult. Assisting students in developing challenging but reachable learning goals enhances their passion for learning, which is a necessary component of grit in providing the motivation to persist through challenges. Students need circumstances to develop grit; it doesn't happen on its own.

To introduce grit in your classroom:

- Define and discuss grit with students.
- Share examples of people who have overcome difficult situations and are great role models for grit.
- Encourage students to read a biography of someone they respect who has overcome great difficulty through long-term effort. Support students in practicing self-compassion when they make mistakes or have failures when learning.
- Talk about someone "gritty" you know, and inspire your students to develop a circle of friends who exhibit grit.

By the way, you may appreciate these strategies as appropriate for adults as well as children. For example, we have shared this approach for many years at Nova Southeastern University's leadership conference with adult students keen to complete their dissertations.

Feedback After Mistakes and Failures

Imagine if all the great inventors and scientists throughout history used failure as an excuse to give up. Would we have electricity? The telephone? The Internet? A cure for polio or other eradicated diseases?

Even the most successful individuals among us have failed at something in life. Resilience, persistence, adaptability, and experimentation have enabled us to move past those failures to find subsequent success. Sometimes, however, keeping students motivated to try in the aftermath of a failure can be challenging for educators and parents.

Students may interpret setbacks or failure as being caused by an inherent lack of ability, in which case they won't be inclined to redouble their efforts so that they can succeed at a similar task the next time. If students attribute their failure to something that is inherent within their being, they are more likely to develop a pessimistic outlook that will thwart successful learning in the future. Teaching students that failure is a temporary setback that can be overcome through the use of effective learning strategies establishes a foundation upon which they can build a sense of mastery that drives practical optimism and self-efficacy.

Educators can help students recast their perceptions about mistakes and setbacks as a normal part of learning by highlighting their own thinking while problem solving aloud. It helps students understand that everyone makes mistakes—and that mistakes help us learn. Figure 4.2 illustrates differing responses to learning—or not learning—from mistakes based on one's mindset.

Kelly Rose, media center director at The Out-of-Door Academy in Sarasota, Florida, explains her strategy for shifting students' and their parents' perceptions regarding mistakes and failures to an opportunity for growth. "When you tell them that mistakes are a way to grow, it does not seem so bad," she explains. "You have to teach parents this as well. This is a mind shift, especially for parents who expect straight As with no excuses." Rose suggests that teachers convey to students that failure at a given task is not due to lack of ability and explain that their performance can be enhanced, particularly with added effort or through the use of different strategies. "Attributing failure to low ability often leads students to give up when they encounter failure," she says. "Hence, when students believe their performance can be improved, they are fostering a growth mindset that can bring motivation and persistence to bear on challenging problems or material" (Wilson & Conyers, 2013a, p. 9).

FIGURE 4.2
Learning/Not Learning from Mistakes

	Fixed Mindset	Growth Mindset
What does failure mean?	Low intelligence—"This is the best I can do."	Low effort or poor strategy —"Next time, I'll work harder and smarter."
What does effort mean?	Low intelligence—"I have to work hard because I'm not smart."	Use and improvement of intelligence—"If I work harder, I'll get smarter."
How does one respond when encountering difficulty?	Less effort—"Why should I try? What's the use?"	More effort—"If at first you don't succeed, try something different or work a little harder."
How does one perform in response to difficulty?	Impaired—"See? I did even worse the second time!"	Equal or improved—"I did better this time, and figured out some things!"

Adapted from Dweck, 2002, p. 41.

Eight Strategies for Giving Feedback After Learning Setbacks

When giving feedback after learning setbacks:

- *Be specific about the skill or area of knowledge that needs improving.* Say, for example, "Let's go over the rubric on writing research papers to focus on organizing the information you want to present."
- *Make feedback personal and tailor it to student's individual needs.* When possible, have private one-on-one sessions

with students, as they provide a safe, focused means of providing feedback. Say, for example, "I found division to be really hard when I was a kid too, so I wanted to share some ideas that helped me understand it better."

- *Deliver feedback promptly so the student will remember the learning task and can more productively apply your guidance.* You can, for example, say something like, "This morning in the reading group, I noticed you skipped over a couple new words. Let's review some clues you can use to figure out the meaning of words like that."

- *When suggesting alternative strategies, emphasize that the student decides how to use your guidance.* You might, for example, say something such as, "Do you have a favorite way to assess yourself? You might consider using a strategy like 'Explain It to Your Brain' [presented later in this chapter] to help prepare for our next quiz."

- *Find at least one positive thing to say about the student's work.* Perhaps say, "It is clear that you care a lot about the subject of your paper."

- *Maintain a positive and encouraging outlook.* Offering feedback with a smile and lighter tone is engaging and helps build a strong teacher–student relationship.

- *Use a variety of modalities in providing feedback, including verbal questions and conversations, written notes, even gestures such as a thumbs-up when a student makes positive progress.* Sticky notes are a handy means of posting feedback at appropriate places on the student's papers, other media, books, and desk; the student can remove a note after addressing the feedback and decide whether to keep it for future reference.

- *Use "I" statements to acknowledge growth and the use of learning strategies.* For example, "I noticed that you have been using a checklist in organizing this latest project. How has that been helpful?"

Growth Assessments

Formative (growth) assessments is a term we use for *formative assessments* that help give students feedback, guide student learning, monitor progress, and increase motivation. There is a positive association overall between the use of formative assessment and student learning. It is most effective when there are clear learning targets, there is feedback regarding where students are in relation to these targets, this feedback is used to adjust instruction and students' learning activities, and it is delivered in a supportive way (National Academies of Sciences, Engineering, and Medicine, 2018, pp. 154–155).

Students benefit when teachers check in often and provide additional instruction and feedback when necessary. This is especially beneficial for students who have learning challenges, as it helps them use teacher feedback for improvement and better stay on a course of growth and success. Growth assessments help students identify their strengths and areas of weakness/that need further practice and reinforcement. Keeping track of their growth, including learning challenges they have overcome, helps students understand how their hard work translates into improvement and fosters a growth mindset.

Measuring what children are learning on an incremental basis and using that information to guide classroom practice supports an understanding of a growth mindset and malleable intelligence. Teachers who share this understanding might use formative assessments to help students achieve their mastery learning goals. Further, these teachers understand that standardized and intelligence tests provide only one piece of information about a student's intelligence. They should not be relied on as the only indicators of a student's ability and should never be used as an excuse for lowering expectations about what students can achieve.

Five Strategies to Facilitate Growth Assessments

To facilitate growth assessments

- *Facilitate class discussions* so that you and students can share strategies that work (this is especially useful when many students have similar weaknesses).
- *Organize interviews* with individual students when necessary.
- *Conduct teacher-student consultations* on drafts of work.
- *Observe* how students are successfully applying what they've learned.
- *Help students use self-assessments* such as journal entries and personal checklists so they can monitor their progress.

Supporting Students' Growth Mindsets

Figure 4.3 summarizes do's and don'ts based on our discussion in this chapter on helping students develop a growth mindset.

Teacher-Tested Technique: Applying Feedback to Steer Learning

Feedback comes from various sources—guidance from teachers, test scores, critiques from peers, and students' self-assessments—but it must be applied effectively to have a positive impact on learning. Educators can use the following techniques to model and guide students in applying feedback to improve learning outcomes.

Explain It to Your Brain

Help students engage in self-assessment by applying a process we call "explain it to your brain" (Wilson & Conyers, 2016a, pp. 84–87). You can teach this skill by modeling self-explanation aloud in the classroom. For example, when working at the board, you might ask yourself a question aloud like, "How might I solve this problem?" Then you could talk through the problem aloud so that students can learn from your modeling how to engage in self-dialogue when reading, problem solving, or engaging in other learning tasks. After they have experienced your modeling across different contexts, give students opportunities to use the strategy aloud (with the goal being for students to use the tool silently and independently).

FIGURE 4.3
Guiding Students to Develop and Sustain a Growth Mindset

Do	Don't
When possible, give students choice based on their interests in what they read and when assigning projects and other learning tasks.	Assign materials and projects to students without taking into account personal interests.
Emphasize learning (mastery) goals that concentrate on what students will know and be able to do as a result of completing a task.	Focus only on performance goals (like getting a certain score) (as such goals, while they can be healthy, should not be at the heart of schooling).
Attribute success to working hard and using appropriate methods.	Attribute success to being smart (which can backfire when students have a difficult task to complete).
Praise students for working hard, using effective strategies, and asking questions when necessary.	Praise students for answering quickly or without trying.
Encourage students to embrace mistakes.	Reinforce students' regret, self-depreciation, and negative self-talk when they make mistakes.

The Next Time (TNT), Step by Step

This strategy is designed to help students develop the habit of focusing in the aftermath of a mistake or setback on what they might do in similar situations in the future to create a better outcome (Wilson & Conyers, 2018). In short, the aim is to turn a failed attempt into a future success. Teachers have told us that this strategy is a powerful way for students to begin to learn from their mistakes and, most importantly, to focus on planning to do things differently the next time. Teaching students this strategy keeps the focus on the process of learning rather than on considering themselves a failure after making a mistake.

Step 1. Explain that The Next Time (TNT) is a dynamic strategy for changing behavior.

Step 2. Tell students that it's common, but not helpful, to feel frustrated when they make a mistake and that a more useful response is to deal with the situation at hand and say, "The next time I will..." Encourage them to see themselves doing something different, notice how they feel about it, and make it real.

Step 3. Practice this process with your students over and over until it becomes automatic.

Step 4. Use this system regularly with your students to help them create change.

Growth Folders, Step by Step

One way to guide students to become self-confident learners who feel good by doing well is to help them to hit the "save key" on their successes. With this approach, you can guide students in building a "growth folder" (Wilson & Conyers, 2018, p. 231) filled with concrete and authentic academic successes they are achieving at school.

A growth folder is a continually updated collection of work that students keep. The contents include materials to help them internalize and remember their learning successes. Keeping track of students' growth, including learning challenges they have overcome, helps foster a growth mindset. Growth folders can help sustain growth mindsets over time.

Step 1. Give every student a folder to use to keep evidence of their learning. (Many teachers we know seem to enjoy using bright yellow folders.)

Step 2. Ask students to write the word *success* on their folder or draw a picture that represents success for them.

Step 3. Each day, when possible, ask students to add to their folders examples of successful learning, such as tasks completed, learning gains, and assignments that support their personal definitions of success.

Step 4. At the start of each school day or class, remind students to look through their success folders. The more students can reconnect to their prior successes, the more positive their mindsets can become and the more successful they'll be in the long run.

Step 5. Periodically, if necessary, remind students that their folders are a way for them to keep track of their learning growth and celebrate their successes.

Teaching Strategies That Sustain Growth Mindsets

Certainly, we want children to appreciate the fruits of hard work.
But we also want them to understand the importance of trying new
strategies when the one they are using isn't working. (We don't
want them to just try harder with the same ineffective strategy.)
                              —Carol Dweck, *Mindset* (2016a, p. 215)

Principle 6: *Improve methods*—like those shared
throughout this book—to increase successful learning
outcomes and sustain a growth mindset over time.

Seeing the classroom environments teachers have created for
actively developing a growth mindset is one of the most gratifying
parts of our work. These classrooms are warm, welcoming, and
lively places that support the kinds of learning opportunities we
wish we had experienced more often when we were students. We
use the term *growth encourager* to describe teachers, coaches, and

mentors who support the growth of others in schools. This chapter explores some of the methods growth encouragers are using to foster positive and productive learning environments where growth mindsets thrive and to teach strategies across multiple learning pathways to enhance academic gains.

Creating Learning Environments Designed for Growth

Teachers who are growth encouragers provide students with many opportunities to learn in optimal environments that support the work of the brain to engage with sustained, flexible attention and to make meaning through emotionally relevant learning. In these classrooms that inspire and expect growth, it is clear that there are high expectations for all students in terms of their personal growth trajectories. Often, when we ask students what they are working on, they clearly describe what their learning goals are and how they are pursuing them. In our work, we use a metaphor comparing curriculum to a road. The reality is that students arrive in the classroom at different points along the road, and they all have great potential for proceeding further in their learning journey.

The key to effective teaching is to create growth experiences and encouragement that help students move along the curriculum road. In the classrooms we visit, we find that students are making steady progress and that mistakes are seen as mere bumps in the road that assist in learning endeavors. Teachers enjoy seeing the lightbulbs switch on as students make learning gains or finally grasp a complex concept. A palpable sense of belonging occurs when students are actively engaged in the learning process and know their teacher cares deeply about their learning. In this type of classroom, students can devote their brains' attention to learning, remembering, and growing.

Fostering Positive Relationships

Classrooms featuring conditions that foster student learning and growth mindsets are most likely to be low-stress environments where students feel safe and accepted. These classrooms emphasize collaboration and personal development rather than competition and comparison with others. In a meta-analysis of 119 studies, Jeffrey Cornelius-White (2007) found that students in these types of classrooms with learner-centered teachers have more respect for themselves and others, are less resistant to and more engaged in learning, and achieve higher outcomes. Teacher–student relationships are enriched, Cornelius-White adds, when teachers model caring and treat each student as a person worthy of respect. This involves making an effort to see students' points of view and communicating them back to students, which not only helps them feel safe but allows them to learn how to self-assess and how to understand other people and content with the same concern and interest.

Modeling respect for others and understanding their perspectives can guide students to develop the core competencies of social and emotional learning. Research indicates that "individuals' brains are critically shaped by social relationships, and the information they learn through these relationships supports both their emotions and their knowledge about facts, procedures, motivation, and interests" (National Academies of Sciences, Engineering, and Medicine, 2018, p. 29).

The interrelationship of emotion and learning is reflected in the words of Georgia coach Maureen Ryan: "We have to remain positive, optimistic, and encouraging. I want students to know I am one of their biggest fans, and I support their creativity, imagination, and dreams for their future success" (Wilson & Conyers, 2013a, p. 34). The adage that students don't care what you know until they know you care applies to fostering a positive and productive learning environment.

Miriam, whom we met in Chapter 2, also exemplifies a teaching approach that emphasizes positive relationships, active engagement, and purposeful learning. Students react positively to the environment, as one view shared by Miriam shows:

> As one of my former language arts connections students said: "I like your class, but not because of friends. I like it because of activities that we do in your class, and I thought I would tell you what I like. I like the daily grammar practice we do because I can interact without the fear of being wrong. In my other language arts class, the fear is always there, so I don't interact with the class. I like doing all the projects in your class with other students on the computer because the students and me can really learn things about each other." (Germuth, 2012, p. 18)

The positive experience recounted by Miriam's student is compatible with research findings showing that teachers can have a significant influence on the nature and establishment of students' friendships (Donohue, Perry, & Weinstein, 2003; Hendrickx, Mainhard, Boor-Klip, Cillessen, & Brekelmans, 2016). For example, elementary school students may accept or reject a peer as a friend based on their perceptions of how their teacher treats the child. If the teacher appears to see a child in a positive light (or conversely, in a negative light), she is likely to be seen in the same way by peers. Teachers like Miriam lead students to care for the feelings of others and exhibit confident learning behaviors in the classroom.

Teachers who embody a growth mindset encourage high levels of learning through student involvement each day. They promote equal participation for all students and foster a feeling of belonging in their classrooms. When students feel respected, accepted, and included in day-to-day activities, they are more likely to participate in and contribute to classroom discussions and group projects—and in the process learn more and achieve at higher levels (Davis & Dague, 2020). A classroom that neglects these aspects of a positive and productive learning environment may have a potentially damaging impact on students' intellectual development and achievement.

Dweck (2016a) contends that educators with a fixed mindset tend to create a judgmental environment. The concern is that these teachers may assess students' performance at the beginning of the school year, deciding which students are smart and which are not, and use those labels as their guide throughout the year—in effect, giving up on the students for whom they have low expectations. On the other hand, teachers with a growth mindset who benefit from learning current research and strategies—those who believe that intelligence is malleable—model this mindset in the classroom and foster growth mindsets among their students, leading to greater student motivation and effort. Working from this mindset, students can become smarter.

While on the Scholars Program selection panel at Carl Albert State College (CASC) assisting with interviews with some 40 students soon to graduate from high school and transition to college, Donna recalls that these self-selected applicants for scholarships often named educators who instilled in them a strong ethic for hard work, completing tasks (academic and otherwise) well, and volunteering to serve others in their communities. The students' stories were shining examples of growth mindsets in action inspired by teachers.

Teachers' Personal Growth Stories

Educators we know often tell their students about their own growth—and their learning from failures and mistakes. In one of our workshops many years ago, a teacher told one such story we have never forgotten. He described how he framed a report card showing an *F* he had earned in school. Naturally, his students asked him why he had framed this bad report card. He replied, "I want you to see that wherever you start, you can always grow."

We use the term *teachers' personal growth stories* to describe such stories, and we believe that teachers who share them can be powerful *growth heroes* that their students can emulate. The following Teacher-Tested Technique offers suggestions on how to uncover your own personal growth stories to help students begin to develop the confidence to share their stories (complete with mistakes) safely and with your encouragement.

When visiting schools, we often have lunch with students. Kids talk! They are clear about the kinds of teachers they want and the learning environments and strategies that help keep them more engaged and motivated. We imagine that, years later, when such a teacher is approached by a former student in the grocery store, the student will say something like, "You really made a difference in my life." Donna heard one such story when she was assisting on the Scholars Program selection panel at CASC: While there, I was introduced to a young woman studying at the college who was quick to credit her kindergarten and 3rd grade teacher, Leslie Wilson, with teaching her to read well and enjoy school. She was so glad she had the opportunity to be taught by Mrs. Wilson for not one but two whole years! It was clear that the support and opportunity to become an independent learner this teacher-in-training received in her early school years helped put her on the road to academic success and inspired her to become a teacher.

Five Strategies to Foster a Positive Growth-Minded Learning Environment

A caring and respectful relationship with their teacher can make a big difference for students. Reflecting on their school days, many describe how a favorite teacher made them feel excited about learning or how they always felt the teacher provided a caring and safe environment where it was OK to make mistakes and where they felt valued as a person.

To foster that environment in your classroom and school

- *Give students a positive greeting when they arrive each day.* This can help students start the day off right. Paying attention to body language, as well as listening to their comments, can also help head off potential problems later in the day.
- *Ask students to do a simple interest inventory by writing down five favorite things they like to do.* Their responses will provide ideas for making the curriculum more relevant to their lives—thus showing students that you care.
- *Spend a couple minutes each day with a struggling student.* Focus on building a positive relationship with the student rather than talking about their learning challenges.
- *Be a role model who shows students how to be empathetic.* As educators demonstrate how to be more understanding and compassionate with others, over time, students mirror thoughtful and caring behaviors.
- *Actively listen to students, attending to the meaning behind what they say before checking in with them to make sure you understand.* This supports students' dignity and helps in the development of a trusting relationship.

Teacher-Tested Technique: Sharing Stories That Illustrate Growth Mindsets

Thanks to their intelligent and malleable brains, students and teachers alike can develop emotions that influence and steer their social and intellectual endeavors, including "admiration to make us emulate the virtue of others" (Immordino-Yang, 2016, p. 18). Stories of heroes and heroines from throughout the centuries in the hands of a growth-minded teacher have the power to inspire heroic thoughts and actions in the minds of young people, as in Marcus's example from "Milo and the Bull": This great story helped shape my perceptions of the world. Milo, a young boy in Greece, began carrying a baby calf on his shoulders as he walked on a long, uphill path every day. The calf grew bigger and bigger every year until it was a full-grown bull. As an adult, Milo's strength and stamina grew to the point that he could carry this full-grown bull on his shoulders. The character of Milo is well recorded in ancient history, and he was a heroic leader who led by example. I first heard this story at school in Cambridge, England, more than 50 years ago, and it still influences me today.

Donna recalls how reading about one of her childhood heroines, Nancy Drew, aided in the development of her budding love of travel and adventures when she was a girl. Effective teachers encourage students to choose the virtuous characters they want to read about and perhaps emulate.

Milo and Nancy Drew are examples of what we call *growth heroes* to refer to people noted for courageous acts or nobility of character. We encourage teachers to amplify stories with growth heroes rather than stories that feature a character who was born a hero and didn't have to learn. For example, we appreciate the skills that *The Karate Kid* needed to learn versus the depictions of *Superman*, who, although beloved by children, had superhuman traits that he didn't have to work to develop. (The Appendix provides a list of books for children and teens with characters and storylines that illustrate a growth mindset.)

Studying Growth Heroes, Step by Step

Growth mindset may be a difficult concept for students to understand and apply in their own lives. Classroom discussions with examples that are relevant and age-appropriate can help students appreciate how a growth mindset can help power up their personal and academic pursuits.

Step 1. Begin with your own personal growth story. Reflect on instances in your own journey of learning when you have had to work hard to overcome a challenge. Begin a discussion on growth mindsets by sharing one of your stories that might inspire your students.

Step 2. Facilitate a discussion about your story and ask students to share examples of learning challenges they have encountered and overcome through a belief that they could succeed through persistence and a belief in their abilities.

Step 3. Tell students that their own examples and experiences with growth mindsets are similar to those of real-life and fictional heroes who exhibited great courage in dealing with learning challenges on their way to achieving their dreams.

Step 4. Assign students a learning project to research and report on their favorite growth heroes. (You can share the books in the Appendix as examples of stories of growth heroes.) If appropriate, encourage students to deliver their project through the medium of their choice, such as a book report, a poster or other visual display that describes their growth hero, or an oral presentation.

Step 5. Upon completion and presentation of the students' growth hero projects, lead a discussion on what their subjects have in common and how students might apply the lessons learned from their research to their own learning.

Multiple Learning Pathways in the Brain

Just as plants grow differently in different gardens, in different climates, and with different types of care, students' brains develop differently depending on "predispositions, priorities, experiences, and environment" (Immordino-Yang et al., 2018, p. 1). To promote the growth of all students, it is important to use multisensory strategies to support more areas of memory storage and more widespread connections among related memory circuits in multiple brain regions. These strategies include creating learning experiences related to visualization, sound, touch (through use of manipulatives), movement, and combinations of these (Willis & Willis, 2020).

The more learning pathways teachers offer throughout the day, the more likely it is that students will learn and remember more. Consider the following examples:

- *Content.* When appropriate, use real experiences, videos, manipulatives, and alternate short presentations with learner-led processes in your lessons.
- *Processes.* Ensure that students have opportunities to work on their own and in various-sized groups. Allow time for student reflection and movement during the day.
- *Products.* Allow students to show how they understand content in a variety of ways on assignments, projects, and tests. For example, students can give a presentation, create an artistic representation, invent something, or write an essay or a poem.

Effective educators provide learning experiences many students enjoy that strengthen different learning pathways. For example, a few popular ideas are filmmaking, fiction writing, inventing, sustainability of the Earth, conscious well-being, music, martial arts, sports, and financial literacy. Notice that many of these examples rely on experiences that engage the body–brain system in learning.

Encouraging Students to Engage in Deliberate Practice

In addition to facilitating multiple learning pathways, teachers can support student learning gains with the reinforcing message that it takes effort to achieve academic success. This message reflects a basic element of developing and sustaining a growth mindset—the need to persist, especially when learning gets tough. Research indicates that hard work is most beneficial if it takes the form of *deliberate practice*—planned activities at a level slightly beyond the currently attainable level of accomplishment that require concentration, include feedback on completion of practice activities, and afterward are improved upon and repeated (Ericsson & Pool, 2016).

The implication for educators is that we should never underestimate the power of practice or assume that a student cannot do something if he has not had the opportunity for extended practice. It is necessary to provide opportunities to practice through creative and innovative tasks, both to accommodate a diverse range of students across a broad range of subjects and to maintain their interest through a variety of methods for processing information (Wilson & Conyers, 2020).

Three Strategies to Support Students' Multiple Learning Pathways

To support students' multiple learning pathways

- *Accommodate students' diverse learning processing preferences* by incorporating a variety of content presentations and learning activities throughout the school day.
- *When possible, give students options* on how to demonstrate what they have learned through written, oral, and artistic projects and presentations that incorporate movement.
- *Encourage deliberate practice across a variety of learning methods* by guiding students to push themselves toward the next level of knowledge and skills, seek feedback on their progress, and continue to repeat and improve upon their learning.

Teacher-Tested Techniques: Sustaining Learning Growth Across Academic Subjects

The following lessons and techniques create growth experiences for students with specific strategies and across learning modalities and academic subjects. Explicit instruction and modeling of these strategies provide great ways for students to see how smart they are after teachers set the stage by introducing the concept of brain plasticity—that learning actually changes the brain (see Chapter 2).

Memory Pegs, Step by Step

This technique exemplifies a learning experience that enhances recall by employing association and the encoding of information using a number of different brain pathways (e.g., visualizing, listening, touching, speaking, and sharing with another). Through the use of this tool, students can effectively simultaneously grow their memory skills while realizing the power of their brilliant brains.

Effective teachers know that it is important for students to develop a deep understanding of important content—and then to apply learning strategies to ensure that this new understanding of core content can be retained, recalled, and applied in academic and other contexts (Wilson & Conyers, 2015). In his theory of successful intelligence, educational researcher Robert Sternberg identifies four distinct thinking skills, all of which can be learned and improved: memory, analytical skills, creative skills, and practical skills. "We start with memory because if you have no information or skills to draw upon, there is nothing to analyze, create, or apply" (Sternberg, Jarvin, & Grigorenko, 2015, p. 19).

Memory Pegs (Wilson & Conyers, 2018, p. 295) is one of the favorite strategies we teach in professional development and at conferences. Teachers who use this tool in their classrooms find that it is highly motivating, leads to positive discussion, and reinforces students' beliefs that they can improve their learning through the use of effective strategies.

We recommend that, initially, you enjoy learning this strategy with a partner—a colleague, friend, spouse, or child. After familiarizing yourself with the strategy, you can then use Memory Pegs as an effective way to support growth mindsets in the classroom by providing an opportunity for students to experience earned success.

As you introduce Memory Pegs in the classroom using the following first three steps, be sure to elicit student conversation. We recommend that you listen for clues about what is going on with students' mindsets. For example, before taking on a learning task that is difficult (like remembering a list of 10 items), self-talk can be quite negative. Continue to listen to their chatter as students then engage and have fun with the task as you teach them the 10 pegs. At this stage, you will probably hear their talk become slightly more positive after you teach them the strategy to assist their memory. Then after the group test, teachers are often pleased to see beaming smiles and positive self-talk. The goal is for the group to experience success by remembering more items through the use of the pegs than without them. The goal is *not* to experience perfection.

Step 1. Ask students to stand in two rows, listen to a list of up to 10 words related to a lesson, and try to remember them all. In an elementary science lesson, for example, the list might include the stars and planets that make up our solar system (see Figure 5.1).

Step 2. Ask students to turn to the person next to them and recite the list of words in order. We like to say that when students work in pairs in growth-minded classrooms, they are *growth buddies*. This term can also be used among teaching colleagues who share growth plans and to provide constructive feedback and celebrate long-term progress.

Step 3. Ask who remembers all 10 words in order, 9 words in order, 8 words in order, 7 words in order, and so on, and keep a tally of how many students remember each number.

Step 4. Ask students if they would like to learn a way to easily remember all 10 words on the list—and apply this strategy to other facts they need to remember.

Step 5. Guide students to mirror you as you tap "pegs" on your body: (1) head, (2) shoulders, (3) heart, (4) belly, (5) hips, (6) backside, (7) thighs, (8) knees, (9) shins, and (10) toes.

Step 6. Tap each peg again, this time associating each with a word on the list.

FIGURE 5.1
Examples of Memory Pegs

Tap each "peg" on your body as you say the next word on the list	**Elementary Science:** The stars and planets in our solar system	**High School Language Arts:** Literary devices
Head	Sun	Allegory
Shoulders	Mercury	Alliteration
Heart	Venus	Aphorism
Belly	Earth	Assonance
Hips	Mars	Hyperbole
Backside	Jupiter	Imagery
Thighs	Saturn	Juxtaposition
Knees	Uranus	Metaphor
Shins	Neptune	Simile
Toes		Symbol

Step 7. Direct students to recall the words in order as they tap their Memory Pegs. Note how many students remembered fewer, the same number, or more of the words this time compared to the first time.

Step 8. Lead a discussion about other situations where the Memory Pegs technique might be handy and about how strategies can help us grow our learning skills. This, in turn, might support the development of a growth mindset.

Step 9. Debrief as part of a discussion on mindsets. You may want to point out your observations of the group's initial concerns and the way the Memory Pegs strategy aided recall and success. Facilitate reflection with the following questions:

- What were you telling yourself about recalling a list of nine or ten words without a strategy?
- What were you saying to yourself after the group test?

- How do you think you will feel facing the next challenging task you have in class where a strategy like this might be useful?

Extender

This strategy can be applied across different content lessons as well as grades. In math, for example, high school students can use Memory Pegs to remember geometry formulas. In elementary language arts, students can improve their recall of the parts of speech. Middle school students can recall elements on the periodic table. Memory Pegs is also a popular strategy in our teacher workshops and offers an easy application to incorporate into your personal and professional toolbox of cognitive strategies. As just one professional example, Memory Pegs can help you recall the components of a lesson—and demonstrate this strategy in action for students.

Marcus has used this strategy to teach key content from the book *The 7 Habits of Highly Effective People* (Covey, Covey, & Collins, 2020). (As only seven pegs are needed, the last body peg is the thighs.) In a personal example, we use this strategy to help us remember various superfoods when we prepare to go to the grocery store and to recall and apply content from a variety of contexts. For more memory strategies, see our article "Put Working Memory to Work in Learning," which can be found at https://www.edutopia.org/blog/put-working-memory-to-work-donna-wilson-marcus-conyers.

Memory Scape, Step by Step

Marcus developed a process we call *memory scaping* (Wilson & Conyers, 2018, pp. 191–193), which uses the power of location memory to map out an event that students need to remember. Here's Marcus's description of the strategy in action: I began testing this strategy in a lesson about the Battle of Waterloo, first teaching it with lecture only, which elicited an audience response of groans and yawns. Then, I "memory-scaped" the battle: Beginning on the right side of the room, I described the red English uniforms and how the soldiers held their muskets and bayonets in front of them as they moved across the field. Next, I physically moved to the left side of the room, where I described the French, dressed in blue, with their black hats, aiming their cannons at the approaching troops. After this, I moved to the back of the room to describe the Prussian cavalry dressed in gray, riding down the hill. Finally, I hurried back to the front of the room to describe the rockets bursting above. When I presented the Battle of Waterloo this way, the students were motivated and engaged in the lesson. They were "hooked" and ready to learn more about this important battle and after further study could more easily recall the details.

Step 1. Decide how to use the classroom space to create an attention-grabbing Memory Scape. For example, in Marcus's history lesson, he divided the classroom space to represent three different locations.

Step 2. Consider appropriate sensory language you want to use to make the lesson memorable.

Step 3. Teach your lesson with enthusiasm.

Step 4. Assess students' memory for the minilesson. After teaching the lesson, move around the room using the same locations you used when you taught the lesson and ask questions. In the lesson Marcus taught, for example, questions might include: "Who fought in this location on the battlefield?" and "What did their uniforms look like?"

Step 5. After using Memory Scape to help generate student interest in key content you teach, follow up with a discussion on the importance of the content and ideas on how students can continue to engage in making meaning based on your introduction.

Extenders

Donna used this same strategy during a keynote for a gathering of the Jamaica Teachers Association, as shown in the YouTube video at https://www.youtube.com/watch?v=Igg_j7re7qE. Notice the educators' active engagement as she provided a brief visual depiction of an introduction to the Battle of Waterloo, resulting in the defeat of Napoleon's forces that ended Napoleon's rule and France's dominance in Europe.

This strategy is adaptable to a variety of topics in diverse settings. Imagine how effective it would be to create a giant Memory Scape in the gymnasium, for example, using string to mark out different countries. Involve the students by asking them to play the leaders of the countries. Also ask them to learn five key facts about the country they are representing. Now imagine each student going for a voyage around the world, learning information from each leader. This system uses motor and episodic memory systems and involves all the senses to facilitate retention and recall.

Educators can build on the interest piqued by the memory scaping technique. To follow up on the initial lesson, ask students to learn more by doing online research, checking out library materials, and seeking out additional resources to further enhance the learning experience.

Chapter Scape

Ask students to demonstrate key elements of a book chapter. This energizing activity gives students practice in clarifying the most important parts of the text and an opportunity to communicate in a format that may be engaging for students with writing challenges. Teachers we know enjoy encouraging their students to dress the part of their character when appropriate and possible. We have seen how—in a moment before, during, or after an enactment—some students with reading challenges begin to believe that they can understand print. Just like that, they can develop a growth mindset for reading.

Talk Show

Pair up students and ask them to choose which of the two will pretend to be a character from a book or a famous scientist or historical figure who will be interviewed by the other, who will play the role of a talk show host. This strategy encourages students to "get into the brain" of the characters they meet in print. Through an expression of interest in a favorite character, students learn from print in meaningful ways. The Talk Show strategy can also be adapted to enable students to interview a favorite author.

Brain Movies, Step by Step

Visualizing scenes and characters in books and other reading materials helps create meaning in the minds of many students. These steps can help struggling and early readers develop the skill of visualizing.

Step 1. Ask students what they imagine when they hear music and sensory-rich language. Many songs evoke strong images and feelings. One of our favorite examples that we use in workshops with teachers is Louis Armstrong's "What a Wonderful World." (Feel free to use a favorite of yours or your students.)

Step 2. Read aloud passages that have rich sensory language and ask students to visualize their own personal Brain Movie of the scene painted by the words.

Step 3. Pair up students and direct them to take turns actively visualizing and describing a scene from a book or favorite room in their home and summarizing the other student's description. The primary purpose of this exercise is to provide active practice in the art of visualizing, which is a key skill in reading for comprehension and retention.

Step 4. When assigning print selections, choose appropriate reading rich in sensory words and remind students to make a movie in their mind to create meaningful reading (Wilson, 2012).

Teaching Math with Relevance in Mind

Jo Boaler (2016) and Marilyn Burns (2015) are among the leading proponents of teaching mathematics within a problem-solving framework through innovative instructional techniques. This more holistic approach stands in contrast to the traditional basic-skills approach that has served as the underpinning of math instruction in many schools for more than a century.

Think for a moment about the ways we use math in our daily lives. We rarely use a calculator or pencil and paper unless a certain level of accuracy is required. When we dine out, we often estimate the tip in our heads. When we travel on long road trips, we calculate approximately where we will need to stop for gas. When we go to the grocery store, many of us mentally add up each purchase and by the time we approach the cashier, we have a fairly accurate running total.

Now consider the way math is typically taught in school, with arithmetic operations presented in isolation from real-life learning. Students are taught how to perform operations and are given practice worksheets out of the context of life experience. The following examples from our work and the classrooms of teachers who've studied with us illustrate a more engaging and relevant way to teach math.

Health math. Our Health Math approach (Conyers & Wilson, 2015a) guides students to grow math skills as they learn to think critically about what they eat and how they exercise. You can adapt aspects of Health Math in your class by assigning learning projects so students can research and apply math skills on topics such as recommended daily calorie consumption, the amount of weekly exercise necessary to maintain a healthy weight, the amount of calories burned by walking one mile, and the amount of calories in various fast foods and beverages.

Consumer math. Georgia elementary teacher D'Jon McNair facilitated an activity to help students hone their math and living skills by going shopping to find the best bargains. His class studied advertising flyers from three stores to compare prices and calculate how much they could save with coupons and two-for-one offers. These lessons can be extended and adapted for middle and high school students to, for example, create meal plans for a week and calculate the cost of those groceries; to develop a household budget; and to calculate the costs of car ownership (loan payments, insurance, gas, maintenance).

Tax math. Secondary teacher Greta, a participant in the BrainSMART ethnographic study, makes her business education classroom more relevant by focusing on student-led and interactive activities versus teacher-led lessons. Greta taught her students how to compute values on the 1040 tax form by allowing them to conduct research on the computer instead of providing the basic information they needed. As she stated, "It was far more successful than when I led them through it" (Germuth, 2012, p. 16).

Deliberate Practice with Index Cards, Step by Step

In this motivating learning strategy, students use index cards to improve their recall of important information with a portable system. Explain to students that this system to record key facts puts them in charge of their learning and can help them develop a growth mindset about their ability to learn and enhance recall through practice at their own pace. Middle school and secondary school teachers have told us this approach works especially well with teens.

Step 1. Stock up on a good quantity of index cards.

Step 2. Create a sample card by writing on one side of the index card a piece of information you'd like the students to remember and on the other side a question that relates to it. For example, on one side of the card, you might write, "The American Civil War started in 1861." On the other side of the card, you might write, "In what year did the American Civil War start?"

Step 3. Direct students to create their own index cards of information gleaned from lessons, textbooks, and other sources.

Step 4. Explain to students that they can carry the index cards with them, and whenever they have a few spare moments—while they're riding the bus or waiting in line, for example—they can go through their cards to improve their memory of important information.

Step 5. Help students understand the benefit of this system. Instruct them to remove the index card from their deck as soon as they know the information.

Step 6. Continually remind students to create learning decks for key information they need to learn and recall.

This simple and powerful learning system puts students in the driver's seat in terms of how quickly they learn information. The act of writing the cards does a great deal to load the information into their memory banks (Wilson & Conyers, 2018).

Extender

When introducing this system, direct students to work in pairs or small groups to quiz each other with the information recorded on their index cards. This exercise engages students by adding a social element to this study strategy.

Inspiring Concept-Based Teaching

Most educators agree that "teaching to the test"—that is, teaching isolated facts and giving students little opportunity to learn deeply—is not the best approach to ensure that students are really learning and developing growth mindsets, especially in the long run. Whereas standardized tests tend to focus on details and facts, a growth-minded educator aims to equip students with an understanding of the important central concepts of core subjects. Immordino-Yang argues that humans "only think deeply about things we care about" (2016, p. 18) and that it is critical for educators to keep emotions front of mind when designing classroom curricula.

A former middle school teacher, Immordino-Yang recommends that educators encourage and assist students to cultivate emotions that influence and drive their intellectual endeavors, curiosity to help them to explore and discover, and "compassion, indignation, interest, and 'flow'" (2016, p. 18). To illustrate, in an example from her own urban classroom comprising many students living in poverty, the teacher-turned-affective neuroscientist describes how her 7th graders benefited from understandings gleaned from their science class in biology and genetics: "I was intrigued that my students' questions and explanations seemed connected to their friendships, home situations, aesthetic tastes, and cultural values. Students' new scientific understanding of natural selection for adaptive traits like dark or light skin seemed to powerfully influence their peer relationships and their own ethnic identities" (p. 17). Classroom discussions connecting scientific research to their personal lives helped fuel students' interest in science, she concludes. We, too, have witnessed students' growing interest when they engage in lessons about their amazing brains (see Chapter 2) and other content they find relevant and important in their lives.

Guiding Students' Learning Through Broad Conceptual Lenses

A final teaching technique that underscores the core concept of this book—guiding students to develop and apply a growth mindset to their learning—involves introducing broad conceptual lenses that students will find engaging and relevant. This approach is based on the idea that teaching is about guiding students to gain deep meaning that can be transferred broadly in academics and life (Erickson, Lanning, & French, 2017). The role of teachers is to teach the broad context of the subject matter and to help students develop the skills they need to understand and apply what they are learning. In other words, the aim of concept-based teaching is to introduce big ideas and guide students in developing the ability to identify the more detailed information they need to apply what they are learning in specific situations.

H. Lynn Erickson and colleagues (2017) note two primary reasons that a conceptual approach to curriculum and instruction has been challenging more traditional teaching methods in recent decades. First, as a practical matter, there is too much to teach as the knowledge bases across disciplines expand. It is simply more efficient for teachers to assist students in understanding higher-level concepts and principles that define the content. As students begin to see patterns and connections among facts, based on their growing understanding of a concept, they can transfer this knowledge across different contexts. This approach is learner-directed, with the expectation that students will proactively expand their understanding by applying and translating basic concepts in specific situations.

Second, students must learn how to think well to succeed in a complex world. With the current rate of scientific and technological advances, students must be equipped to keep learning so they can adapt to the changing world in which they will live and work. Erickson and colleagues (2017) observe that neither conceptual thinking nor creative, critical, or reflective thinking can be assumed to be a byproduct of factual learning. According to the authors, there is an advantage to intentionally designing into curricular and instructional programs specific requirements to think at higher levels, as it reinforces education as an intellectual process.

Suggestions for looking at topics through conceptual lenses that students may find interesting and relevant, in keeping with the concept-based teaching approach, are presented in Figure 5.2.

FIGURE 5.2
Looking at Topics Through Conceptual Lenses

Topic	Possible Conceptual Lens
Structures in the Brain	Our Brain's Potential (lesson ideas, Chapter 2)
Global Warming	Sustainability of planet Earth
The Food Pyramid	Wellness and Optimistic Living
Thinking Skills	Becoming Lifelong Learners
Assigned Reading	Traveling My Journey of Learning

Conclusion

We have the privilege of writing this book because there were teachers when we were in school who contributed to the development of our own growth mindsets. This allowed us to get way beyond what we thought we were capable of thinking and doing. As an educator reading this book, you have probably already been sowing the seeds of this hope and belief, which may transform the lives of your students in the future. Indeed, teachers have told us about occasions when they were out in their communities and students came up to them to say, "I want to let you know that you really changed my life by believing in me and helping me understand that I can do better than I did before."

Our hope with this book is that we have shared ways for helping even more of your students develop growth mindsets and acquire learning strategies that can help them reach more of their unique potential. As you create new professional goals to do so, remember the words of one of Donna's mentors, Reuven Feuerstein: "As you teach it, you will better learn it. It will come back to you!" Over time, as we have taught using the principles shared in this book, we have gone from a fixed to a growth mindset across a number of contexts.

As you move further in the direction of your dreams, be aware of an approach to life that can limit your growth trajectory over time. This common problem includes falling into the trap of comparing yourself with images of perfection on TV, in movies, and across the Internet, or of expecting to be perfect at something prior to doing the necessary work to acquire the knowledge and skills needed to perform at a high level. A far more useful approach is to focus on making steady progress over time, while celebrating key incremental steps forward, all while cherishing who you are and what goals you wish to pursue.

In our journey together through this book, we have explored the knowledge and methods from a number of research streams that are connected to the process of developing and sustaining growth mindsets. Findings from educational, cognitive, developmental, and positive psychology; from cognitive, developmental, and affective neuroscience; and from educational research on effective instruction and teaching practices support the fundamental principles that form the framework for this book. We have shared many methods that our program graduates have found support positive results in their classrooms, including original strategies we have developed based on what teachers told us was essential for student learning.

While our primary focus has been on supporting teachers help students develop growth mindsets in the classroom setting, we encourage you to use these methods in your professional learning communities, district and school meetings, and more informal learning opportunities. In addition, sharing these ideas and strategies with parents reinforces key concepts and the use of learning strategies at home.

We always finish our live workshops with a growth experience we call the Royal Roundup. Participants are often stunned at how much has been learned and applied during the event! This is a powerful way for all learners to experience and celebrate the growth in their knowledge and skills. Here is a Royal Roundup of our principles, methods, and strategies for developing and sustaining growth mindsets among students and educators alike.

FIGURE C.1
Wilson and Conyers' Seven Principles for
Developing and Sustaining Growth Mindsets

7. Focus on progress,
not perfection

6. Improve methods

5. Get the
feedback needed

4. Set growth goals

1. Understand the
mindsets

2. Keep plasticity
front of mind

3. Learn with
practical optimism

Growth
Mindsets

Principle 1: *Understand the mindsets* so that awareness is maintained with regard to which mindset one is engaged in and what impact it has on motivation and performance.

Chapter 1 presents the following methods and strategies:

- Understand the importance of fixed and growth mindsets in terms of successful learning.
- Recognize examples of a false growth mindset.
- Discover the value of growth mindsets in the classroom.
- Appreciate the link between self-awareness and mindsets.
  —Discover your mindset by reviewing Dwek's statements.
  —Become acquainted with Donna's journey from a fixed to growth mindset.
- Apply the ABC model to examine the impact of fixed and growth mindsets.
  —Be aware of the *assumptions* of each mindset.
  —Be aware of the *behaviors* that occur as a result of each mindset.

—Be aware of the *consequences* that result from the behaviors connected to each mindset.

Principle 2: *Keep plasticity front of mind* as a scientific foundation for developing growth mindsets. Understanding that learning changes the brain can increase motivation.

Chapter 2 presents these methods and strategies:

- Learn how current research about the brain's amazing plasticity forms a neuroscientific understanding of the growth mindset.
  —Explore brain studies linking mindsets, mistakes, and learning.
- Discover the four core factors that power brain growth and lifelong learning.
  —Understand the importance of experiences and environment for learning.
- Acquire four foundational methods for developing brain connections.
  —Create novel learning experiences in the classroom.
  —Challenge students to learn at higher levels.
  —Provide a variety of ways for learners to practice using new knowledge and skills.
  —Give students constructive feedback regarding their progress.
- Become skilled at teaching lessons about the power of the human brain for learning.
  —Teach students the simple fist model of the three-part brain.
  —Share with students a model illustrating how connections are made in the brain.
  —Teach students how they can learn much more than they think, that neuroplasticity is a powerful asset, and that it can power study strategies for successful learning.

Principle 3: *Learn with practical optimism* as an approach to support a growth mindset through increased engagement, focused energy, and resilience in the face of challenges.

Chapter 3 presents the following methods and strategies:

- Discover research on how emotions are the gateway to learning.
- Appreciate an introduction to positive psychology.
  —Consider the 3 *P*s when helping students develop an optimistic attitude.
  —Model an optimistic attitude about learning for students to emulate.
- Assist students in benefiting from positive self-talk.
- Apply strategies to help students become more resilient in the face of challenges.
- Teach students simple tools to use habitually that help them become more optimistic about learning.
- Help students recognize and manage stress and negative feelings.
- Use strategies for incorporating physical activity at school to increase students' positive focus and energy for learning.
  —Illustrate the power of practical optimism with the High-Five activity.
  —Apply the Ball Toss activity to engage students in a fun activity to reinforce learning.

Principle 4: *Set growth goals* and establish targets with a level of challenge that is not too easy or too difficult.

Chapter 4 presents the following methods and strategies:

- Understand motivation as a force that inspires people to set important goals and maintain the drive to accomplish difficult tasks.
- Help students understand the benefits of goal setting.
- Establish high expectations and help students reach appropriately challenging goals.

—Assist students in defining challenging and accessible learning (mastery) goals.

—Give students choices in the content of their projects, reading, and activities when possible.

—Model and discuss how you set goals in your interactions with students.

—Discuss how you can achieve big goals by using small steps and celebrating small wins along the way.

Principle 5: *Get the feedback needed* to continuously improve learning and sustain a growth mindset.

Chapter 4 presents the following methods and strategies:

- Facilitate an understanding that outcomes can be changed for the better by giving students hope that they'll be able to succeed by working harder or trying a different strategy.
- Assist students in developing an internal locus of control with regard to learning outcomes.
- Praise effort rather than ability.
- Define and discuss the importance of grit.
- In response to classroom learning challenges, facilitate a discussion of people who exhibit grit who your students may know or have "met" in their readings.
- Teach students a selection of strategies for developing grit and willpower.
- Use growth assessments to guide students in making incremental learning gains.
- Help students understand that mistakes and failures are temporary setbacks that can be overcome through the use of effective strategies.

  —Guide students to engage in self-assessment by using the Explain It to Your Brain technique.

  —Teach students the The Next Time strategy as a way to learn from their mistakes and focus on planning to do things differently the next time.

—Apply the Growth Folders strategy as a tool to help all students appreciate their growth.

Principle 6: *Improve methods*—like those shared throughout this book—to increase successful learning outcomes and sustain a growth mindset over time.

Chapter 5 presents the following additional methods and strategies:

- Create learning environments designed for growth.
    —Share your personal growth stories as a way to relate to students about overcoming learning challenges and guide them to discover growth heroes who exemplify growth mindsets.
- Foster positive relationships illustrating caring and respect.
    —Design your classroom to place an emphasis on belonging and personal development so that students can learn and grow.
- Provide a variety of opportunities for students to use their brain's multiple pathways to increase the likelihood for learning throughout the school day.
- Give students numerous opportunities for deliberate practice.
- Use learning experiences that rely on a variety of interesting ways to process information across content, processes, and products.
    —Apply tools such as the Memory Pegs technique to give students opportunities to realize their potential to learn and remember.
    —Use Memory Scape to foster student engagement and curiosity to learn more.
    —Use Chapter Scape as a novel way for students to demonstrate key elements of a book chapter.
    —Apply the Talk Show strategy to encourage students to more deeply understand the characters they "meet" in print.

—Teach students to make Brain Movies to help them create personal meaning from print.

—Understand the importance of teaching math with relevance in mind.

—Introduce the use of notes on index cards as a helpful and versatile strategy for deliberate practice to improve recall.

—Discover a concept-based teaching approach that frames content through a broad lens that students may experience as relevant to their lives.

Principle 7: *Focus on progress, not perfection*, and celebrate incremental gains.

Maintaining an awareness of steady improvement fuels a growth mindset over the long haul, as emphasized in discussions and examples presented throughout this book and in this Conclusion.

*   *   *   *   *

In closing, we would like to offer our heartfelt appreciation for all you have done and will do to develop the growth mindsets and learning strategies of your students. These are the game-changing gifts that keep on giving and can make a positive difference throughout students' lives.

Appendix

This additional content and these supplemental exercises and sample lessons are presented to support your understanding and application of the fundamental concepts explored in this text.

A. Our BrainSMART® Approach

Beginning in 1998, a key question that has guided the research and development of our BrainSMART approach shared in this text, professional development, and graduate programs for teachers and administrators is "What research, theory, and concepts on how people learn have high value in terms of their potential for improving teaching practice and student learning?" As we have collected these elements through the years, we have considered the Pareto Principle, popularized as the 80/20 Principle (Koch, 2014), which can be interpreted to mean that the best 20 percent of what has been discovered yields 80 percent of the results. In other words, knowing that all research and theories are not equal, we share what is likely to support teachers most effectively. Furthermore, we share many of our original strategies as part of our methods because we know that busy teachers often do not have time to create their own.

The methods we've developed that we have shared in this book come primarily from research in psychology, neuroscience, and education. The first edition of our text, *Five Big Ideas for Effective Teaching: Connecting Mind, Brain, and Education Research to Classroom Practice* (Wilson & Conyers, 2020), is noted as one of three books that set forth a new type of teacher education based on principles from the transdisciplinary domain of mind, brain, and education science (Tokuhama-Espinosa, 2017). Educators who have studied with us speak enthusiastically about the difference this approach has made for their students and their own professional growth. Our approach relies on innovative applications of a number of research streams that have amassed over decades. Although the References at the end of this book include many excellent examples, what follows are a few we would like to highlight.

Psychology

Several preeminent 20th century researchers and psychologists have made the case that it is possible to help all children improve their intelligence through education. Earlier in this book, you met one of Donna's mentors, the late Israeli psychologist Reuven Feuerstein, who inspired her to believe that intelligence grows as people learn. Early in his career, Feuerstein worked with the Swiss psychologist Jean Piaget, whom many readers will recall from their teacher education. Piaget and Bärbel Inhelder (1972) wrote about the state of disequilibrium that learners experience when contending with new ideas. Central to Piaget's understanding was that disequilibrium led to higher levels of thinking.

In Donna's training to become a psychologist, as she and her fellow students learned how to use various assessments, they studied how Alfred Binet and Theodore Simon conducted research related to developing the cognition of young people who were not benefiting from Paris public schools. Eventually, the duo's development of the Binet-Simon Scale far overshadowed this work, perhaps due to the advent of World War I and a perceived need for mass testing of individuals to see if they were mentally fit to serve in the military. Binet and Simon's pioneering work, revised by Stanford psychologist Lewis M. Terman to become the Stanford-Binet Intelligence Scales, is widely regarded as the precursor to many of today's modern intelligence tests (International Association for Cognitive Education and Psychology, 2016). Piaget, Binet, and Simon, as well as many others whom we rely on in our work, had a common belief that intelligence was not a fixed entity but rather something that could be improved through interventions. In essence, they believed in a growth mindset.

Positive psychology, another research stream that is featured prominently in our work, was officially launched in 1998 when pioneer Martin Seligman was elected president of the American Psychological Association and made positive psychology the year's theme. He became known as one of the five "founding fathers" of positive psychology (PositivePsycology.com, 2019). We have infused knowledge and ideas gleaned from Seligman's research into our BrainSMART approach. Specifically, in this text, you see BrainSMART methods for increasing students' emotional connections to learning, our seminal strategies for helping students become more practically optimistic, and ways in which positive learning environments foster hope, engagement in learning, and resilience.

Neuroscience and Education

Throughout this book, we have included research from several areas of neuroscience to which we often refer. First and central to an understanding of malleable intelligence and growth mindsets is neuroplasticity. In fact, our graduates share that teaching students about their brilliant brains and the potential they have for learning makes an enormous difference in students' motivation to learn. Second, we introduce readers to a researcher in affective neuroscience and former teacher, Mary Helen Immordino-Yang, and share her thinking on how emotions play a key role in human learning (2016). Educational researchers Hattie and Anderman identified factors that have the greatest impact on student achievement, based on a review of hundreds of meta-analyses (2020). They are two of many who study education on whom we rely for assistance as we identify the most important streams that can support teachers.

B. Additional Mindset Assessments

B.1 Professional Mindset "Assessment" for Educators

Adapting Dweck's "assessment" on one's intellectual mindset presented in Chapter 1, we offer this self-check on your teaching and learning mindset:

- You are a certain kind of teacher, and you really can't do much to change that.
- No matter what kind of a teacher you are now, you can change your attitude and approach to teaching substantially.
- You can use some different teaching strategies, but the important parts of who you are as a teacher will remain unchanged.
- You can change how you teach, how you think about teaching, and how you feel about teaching.

In our example, the first and third statements represent a fixed mindset about teaching, while the second and fourth statements represent a growth mindset about your teaching and the profession.

B.2 Exploring Your Personality Mindset

In Chapter 1, we share Dweck's finding that in addition to the development of our "intelligence mindset," personal qualities can also be developed. Dweck calls personality or character propensity the "personality mindset" (2016a). Related to this view, the VIA Character Strengths Survey can guide you to discover your strengths so that you can choose to apply them more frequently in more contexts with the goal of improving performance over time.

The VIA Survey

The VIA Character Strengths Survey is a simple self-assessment that takes most people less than 15 minutes and provides information to help you understand some of your core personality characteristics. This survey, developed by Seligman and Christopher Peterson, distinguished scientist at the University of Michigan and author of *A Primer in Positive Psychology*, focuses on your best qualities rather than on negative and neutral traits as some personality tests do. Seligman theorizes that the 24 VIA character strengths are the pathways to each of the five areas of well-being he articulates in his PERMA model. The five areas that can be enhanced through the use of signature strengths are

- **P**ositive emotion
- **E**ngagement
- **R**elationships
- **M**eaning
- **A**ccomplishments

To take the free survey, go to http://www.viacharacter.org.

C: Selected "Growth Mindset" Reading List for Children and Teens
Ages 4–8

Brave Irene by William Steig—Irene, the loyal young daughter of a dressmaker, perseveres through the wind, cold, and many dangerous obstacles to deliver her mother's work to the duchess.

This inspiring story shows the power of motivation in accomplishing great things.

Everyone Can Learn to Ride a Bicycle by Chris Raschka—This tale of a little girl learning to ride a bike is a relatable milestone for every child. Through practice and determination, and overcoming her frustration, the heroine ultimately prevails.

The Girl Who Never Made Mistakes by Mark Pett and Gary Rubinstein—The titular character is 9-year-old Beatrice, who prides herself on perfection in everything she does. Then one day, she makes a mistake—and everyone in town knows about it. The story conveys that learning from our mistakes can open doors to creativity and even fun.

Flight School by Lita Judge—Penguin has huge dreams of soaring through the sky with the seagulls. Although his body is not in the least designed for flight, Penguin's ingenuity, creativity, and persistence lead to the fulfillment of his dreams. An ideal story for inspiring kids to think creatively.

Hana Hashimoto, Sixth Violin by Chiere Uegaki—Hana is anxious about playing her violin in the talent show, wanting to make beautiful music just like her grandfather in Japan. Though only a beginner, she practices hard so that she can play her best. This story offers hope and confidence to all children who are striving to master a challenging new skill and teaches that there is more than one way to succeed at a given task.

How to Catch a Star by Oliver Jeffers—A young stargazer comes up with many creative attempts to catch a star of his very own and learns that sometimes making your dreams come true requires a little flexibility. This is an inspirational story for encouraging kids to never give up on their dreams.

I Can't Do That, YET by Esther Cordova—This read-aloud book focuses on the importance of the word "yet" in developing a growth mindset. The main character imagines versions of herself in the future and realizes that, with hard work and dedication, she can reach her desired goals.

Jabari Jumps by Gaia Cornwall—Little Jabari is pretty sure—well, he is sort of sure—that he's ready and able to jump off the diving board. After ample reflection and lots of stall tactics, he discovers the courage to face his fears and finally take the leap.

The Life and Art of Horace Pippin by Jen Bryant—This creatively illustrated story tells the tale of a capable artist who grows up absorbed in the joy of creating art, until he is injured in a war. Patiently and with great grit, he slowly regains some of the control in his wounded arm. Although his capabilities aren't the same as before, he becomes an admired artist.

Ages 9–12

Anne of Green Gables by Lucy M. Montgomery—When we traveled in Canada, Donna enjoyed visiting the home of the perpetually optimistic Anne Shirley who, when faced with setbacks, always chooses to try harder to succeed. For her insatiable curiosity, grit, and willingness, Anne has become a cherished character.

Strong Is the New Pretty by Kate T. Parker—The book is a celebration of girls being themselves, as shown through more than 175 photographs. The author helps break stereotypes by showing that girls can be loud, silly, fearless, confident, strong—in other words, whatever they want to be.

Thanks for the Feedback, I Think by Julia Cook—Featuring inventive illustrations, this book follows a day in the life of RJ as he receives feedback, both positive and negative, from his friends, teacher, and parents. At first, RJ is confused about what to do with all this commentary on his skills and behaviors, but he soon learns that feedback is a good thing that will help him improve and grow.

Your Fantastic Elastic Brain by JoAnn Deak—With whimsical illustrations and engaging text, this book explains to young readers how a brain does all the things that "make you YOU." It describes why the brain is the most important organ in the body and gives readers the exciting knowledge that through their actions and efforts, they can help their brain grow.

Wonder by R. J. Palacio—This book shares the inspiring tale of 10-year-old August Pullman, who was born with a rare cranio-facial disorder. After several years of homeschooling Auggie, his parents decide they should no longer shield him from the world around him and enroll him in a mainstream school. Told from multiple points of view, the story provides lessons about empathy, compassion, and perseverance in the face of life's challenges.

Ages 12+

The Boy Who Harnessed the Wind by William Kamkwamba—This memoir recounts how the author saves his family's crops after a drought devastates their tiny Malawi village. After pouring through the science books in the village library, the teenage William comes up with a solution: build a windmill. Not only does the windmill power a water pump for use in the family's farmland, but it also brings electricity to the village. This story shows how great ideas sometimes come from unlikely sources and how the desire to learn can light up the world.

Holes by Louis Sachar—An unlucky boy named Stanley Yelnats is wrongly sentenced to a juvenile detention camp, where he and his fellow inmates are forced to dig holes all day. This darkly humorous tale follows Stanley as he unravels the mystery of why the warden insists that they dig holes and uses his ingenuity to lift an ancient family curse and clear his name.

The House on Mango Street by Sandra Cisneros—This coming-of-age tale follows a year in the life of a 12-year–old Latina girl. Esperanza's journey from girlhood to womanhood gives her a greater understanding of who she is and what she wants to become.

Kira-Kira by Cynthia Kadohata—Katie Takeshima, the middle child in a Japanese American family growing up in post–World War II America, experiences the pain of racial bigotry. Her sister teaches her the Japanese word *kira-kira*, which means glittery and shiny. After suffering a devastating loss, Katie perseveres by using kira-kira to focus on what is bright and hopeful in the world.

A Series of Unfortunate Events by Lemony Snicket (pen name of Daniel Handler)—This popular 13-book series follows the lives of the orphaned Baudelaire children, who must thwart the dastardly Count Olaf's attempts to steal their inheritance. Readers will enjoy figuring out the intricacies of the plot as the children outwit their evil relative through creative problem solving and teamwork.

Their Eyes Were Watching God by Zora Neale Hurston—The novel follows Janie, a black woman who struggles to control her own destiny through the course of her three marriages from her teens into her forties. Published in 1937, the novel has been recognized as a groundbreaking work that shows the importance of finding one's voice and achieving self-actualization.

Unbroken by Laura Hillenbrand—This nonfiction story chronicles the story of Louis Zamperini, who went from troubled teen to Olympic athlete to a World War II veteran who survived a plane crash and a Japanese prisoner-of-war camp. His story shows the resilience of the human spirit and the potential to rise above troubled circumstances.

Growth Glossary

- -

Achievement goal orientation theory. A set of beliefs that reflect how learners approach and engage in academic tasks and influence learning motivation, attitudes, and behavior; see also *performance goal orientation* and *mastery (learning) goal orientation.*

Angiogenesis. The development of new blood vessels that help maintain the blood supply to the brain.

Attribution theory. A concept proposed by Bernard Weiner (1992, 2018) on how people explain their own successes or failures, particularly in terms of achievement, based on three factors—locus of control, stability, and controllability.

Axon. A long, unbranched fiber on a neuron that carries nerve impulses away from one cell to the next cell.

Body-brain system. The ways in which the body and brain work together to support learning.

Brain stem. One of three major parts of the brain; it receives sensory input and monitors vital functions such as heartbeat, body temperature, and digestion.

Cell body. The part of a neuron that contains the nucleus and cytoplasm.

Controllability. A factor associated with attribution theory regarding whether learners believe they can control the cause of outcomes.

Cortex (also referred to as the cerebral cortex). The largest part of the brain; associated with thought and action.

Deliberate practice. Planned learning activities at a level slightly beyond the currently attainable level of accomplishment that require concentration, include feedback on completion of practice activities, and are continually repeated and improved upon.

Dendrite. A branched extension from the cell body of a neuron that receives impulses from nearby neurons through synaptic contacts.

Executive function. A set of cognitive processes that occur in the brain to organize thoughts and activities, set priorities, manage time, and accomplish goals.

Experience-dependent synaptogenesis. The formation of synaptic connections that occur in response to one's experiences and environment; the direct result of learning through one's senses, activities, and thinking processes.

Fixed mindset. The belief that one's personality, intellectual capacity, and abilities are static and largely unchangeable.

Flow. A term adopted by Mihaly Csikszentmihalyi (2008) to describe an optimal psychological state that people experience when they are engaged in an activity that is interesting, engaging, and appropriately challenging.

Formative (growth) assessment. An evaluation that helps guide student learning, monitor progress, and increase motivation to make continued learning gains.

Grit. Perseverance and passion to achieve long-term goals.

Growth mindset. The belief that intellect and other abilities can be developed and improved.

Limbic system. Structures at the base of the brain that control emotions.

Locus of control. A factor associated with attribution theory regarding whether learners believe their success or failure is based on an internal or external cause.

Malleable intelligence. The concept that intellectual capacity is dynamic and changeable as the result of learning.

Mastery (learning) goal orientation. A focus on task completion and understanding, learning, solving problems, and developing new skills.

Metacognition. Thinking about one's thinking with the goal of enhancing learning.

Myelination. The production of a substance in the brain called myelin that insulates and supports neural connections.

Neurogenesis. The creation of new neurons, or brain cells, which occurs across the human lifespan.

Neuron. The basic cell of the brain and nervous system.

Neuroplasticity (also referred to as neural plasticity). The capacity of the brain to change over the lifespan as a result of one's learning, thoughts, and sensory input.

Performance goal orientation. The tendency to approach learning tasks with a focus on how others view one's personal ability, a desire for public recognition for performance, and a need to avoid looking incompetent.

Positive psychology. The scientific study of the strengths that enable individuals and communities to thrive.

Potential. The neurocognitive capacity for acquiring the knowledge, skills, and attitudes to achieve a higher level of performance in any domain.

Practical optimism. An approach to learning and life that focuses on taking practical positive action and supporting positive learning states to increase the probability of successful outcomes.

Pruning. The elimination of neural connections in the brain that are not reinforced with regular stimuli.

Resilience. The quality that allows students who experience learning difficulties and setbacks to persist and continue to strive toward positive outcomes.

Social and emotional learning. Instruction aimed at guiding students to develop competencies to recognize and manage emotions, set and achieve positive goals, appreciate others' perspectives, establish and maintain positive relationships, make responsible decisions, and handle interpersonal situations constructively.

Stability. A factor associated with attribution theory regarding whether learners think the cause of success or failure is likely to remain the same every time or will vary and produce a different outcome the next time.

Synapse. The gap between the axon of one neuron and the dendrite of another; the juncture point where neurons interact.

Synaptogenesis. The formation of neural connections between brain cells to facilitate electric transmissions that aid in cognitive processes such as memory formation and retrieval.

References

American Psychological Association. (2015). Top 20 principles from psychology for preK–12 teaching and learning. Retrieved from http://www.apa.org/ed/schools/cpse/top-twenty-principles.pdf

Ames, C., & Archer, J. (1988). Achievement goals in the classroom: Students' learning strategies and motivation processes. *Journal of Educational Psychology, 80*(3), 260–267. Retrieved from http://citeseerx.ist.psu.edu/viewdoc/download?doi=10.1.1.536.9309&rep=rep1&type=pdf

Anderman, L.H., & Sayers, R. (2020). Academic motivation and achievement in classrooms. In J. Hattie & E. M. Alderman (Eds.), *Visible learning: Guide to student achievement* (pp. 166–172). New York: Routledge.

Anderson, M. (2016) *Learning to choose, choosing to learn.* Alexandria, VA: ASCD.

Aronson, J., Fried, C. B., & Good, C. (2002). Reducing the effects of stereotype threat on African American college students by shaping theories of intelligence. *Journal of Experimental Social Psychology, 38*(2), 113–125.

ASCD. (2018). Teaching students to drive their brains [Video series], featuring Donna Wilson. Retrieved from http://www.ascd.org/professional-development/videos/teaching-students-to-drive-their-brains-videos.aspx

Association for Psychological Science. (2011, September 29). How your brain reacts to mistakes depends on your mindset. Retrieved from https://www.psychologicalscience.org/news/releases/how-the-brain-reacts-to-mistakes.html

Blackwell, L., Trzesniewski, K., & Dweck, C. S. (2007). Implicit theories of intelligence predict achievement across an adolescent transition: A longitudinal study and an intervention. *Child Development, 78*(1), 246–263.

Boaler, J. (2016). *Mathematical mindsets: Unleashing students' potential through creative math, inspiring messages, and innovative teaching.* San Francisco: Jossey Bass.

Boman, P., Furlong, M. J., Shochet, I., Lilles, E., & Jones, C. (2009). Optimism and the school context. In R. Gilman, E. S. Huebner, & M. J. Furlong (Eds.), *Handbook of positive psychology in school* (pp. 51–64). New York: Routledge.

Burns, M. (2015). *About teaching mathematics* (4th ed.). Sausalito, CA: Math Solutions.

Centers for Disease Control and Prevention. (2010, April). *The association between school-based physical activity, including physical education, and academic performance.* Retrieved from www.cdc.gov/healthyyouth/health_ and_academics/pdf/pa-pe_paper.pdf

Claro, S., Paunesku, D., & Dweck, C. S. (2016). Growth mindset tempers the effects of poverty on academic achievement. *Proceedings of the National Academy of Sciences of the United States of America, 113*(31), 8664–8668.

Conyers, M. A., & Wilson, D. L. (2015a). *Positively smarter: Science and strategies for increasing happiness, achievement, and well-being.* Chichester, West Sussex, UK: Wiley.

Conyers, M. A., & Wilson, D. L. (2015b, May). Smart moves: Powering up the brain with physical activity. *Kappan, 96*(8), 38–42. Retrieved from http://www.kappancommoncore.org/wp-content/uploads/2015/04/38pdk_96_8.pdf

Conyers, M. A., & Wilson, D. L. (n.d.). The effects of a positive mindset on school culture. *edCircuit.* Retrieved from https://www.edcircuit.com/effects-positive-mindset-school-culture

Cornelius-White, J. (2007). Learner-centered teacher-student relationships are effective: A meta-analysis. *Review of Educational Research, 77*(1), 113–143.

Covey, S.R., Covey, S., & Collins. J. (2020). *The 7 habits of highly effective people* (30th anniversary ed.) New York: Simon & Schuster.

Csikszentmihalyi, M. (2008). *Flow: The psychology of optimal experience.* New York: Harper & Row.

Damasio, A. R. (1994). *Descartes' error: Emotion, reason, and the human brain.* New York: Putnam.

Davidson, R. J., with Begley, S. (2012). *The emotional life of your brain: How its unique patterns affect the way you think, feel, and live—and how you can change them.* New York: Hudson Street Press.

Davis, H. A., & Dague, C.T. (2020). Teacher-student relationships. In J. Hattie & E. M. Anderman (Eds.), *Visible learning: Guide to student achievement* (pp. 153–159). New York: Routledge.

Dehaene, S. (2020). *How we learn: Why brains learn better than any machine...for now.* New York: Viking.

Donohue, K. M., Perry, K. E., & Weinstein, R. S. (2003). Teachers' classroom practices and children's rejection by their peers. *Journal of Applied Developmental Psychology, 24*(1), 91–118.

Draganski, B., Gaser, C., Kempermann, G., Kuhn, H. G., Winkler, J., Büchel, C., & May, A. (2006). Temporal and spatial dynamics of brain structure changes during extensive learning. *The Journal of Neuroscience, 26*(23), 6314–6317. Retrieved from http://dx.doi.org/10.1523/JNEUROSCI.4628-05.2006

Duckworth, A. L., Peterson, C., Matthews, M. D., & Kelly, D. R. (2007). Grit: Perseverance and passion for long-term goals. *Journal of Personality and Social Psychology, 92*(6), 1087–1101. doi: 10.1037/0022-3514.92.6.1087

Duckworth, A. L., Quirk, A., Gallop, R., Hoyle, R. H., Kelly, D. R., & Matthews, M. D. (2019). Cognitive and noncognitive predictors of success. *Proceedings of the National Academy of Sciences, 116*(47), 23499–23504. doi:10.1073/pnas.1910510116

Duerden, E. G., & Laverdure-Dupont, D. (2008). Practice makes cortex. *The Journal of Neuroscience, 28*(35), 8655–8657.

Durlak, J. A., Weissberg, R. P., Dymnicki, A. B., Taylor, R. D., & Schellinger, K. B. (2011). The impact of enhancing students' social and emotional learning: A meta-analysis of school-based universal interventions. *Child Development, 82*(1). Retrieved from https://casel.org/wp-content/uploads/2016/01/meta-analysis-child-development-1.pdf

Dweck, C. S. (2002). Messages that motivate. In J. Aronson (Ed.), *Improving academic achievement: Impact of psychological forces on education* (pp. 37–60). San Diego: Elsevier.

Dweck, C. S. (2016a). *Mindset: The new psychology of success* (updated ed.). New York: Ballantine.

Dweck, C. S. (2016b, January 13). What having a "growth mindset" actually means. *Harvard Business Review*. Retrieved from https://hbr.org/2016/01/what-having-a-growth-mindset-actually-means

Dweck, C. S. (2019). The choice to make a difference. *Perspective in Psychological Science, 14*(1), 21–15.

Dweck, C. S., & Leggett, E. L. (1988). A social-cognitive approach to motivation and personality. *Psychological Review, 95*(2), 256–273.

Elliot, A. J., & Hulleman, C. S. (2017). Achievement goals. In A. Elliot, C. Dweck, & D. Yeager (Eds.), *Handbook of competence and motivation: Theory and application* (2nd ed., pp. 43–60). New York: Guilford Press.

Erickson, H. L., Lanning, L. A., & French, R. (2017). *Concept-based curriculum and instruction for the thinking classroom* (2nd ed.). Thousand Oaks, CA: Corwin Press.

Ericsson, K. A., & Pool, R. (2016). *Peak: Secrets from the new science of expertise.* Boston, MA: Houghton Mifflin Harcourt.

Fotuhi, M. (2013). *Boost your brain: The new art and science behind enhanced brain performance.* New York: HarperOne.

Fredericks, J., McColskey, W., Meli, J., Mordica, J., Montrosse, B., & Mooney, K. (2011). *Measuring student engagement in upper elementary through high school: A description of 21 instruments* (Issues & Answers Report, REL 2011–098). Washington, DC: U.S. Department of Education, Institute of Education Sciences, National Center for Education Evaluation and Regional Assistance, Regional Educational Laboratory Southeast.

Fredrickson, B. (2009). *Positivity: Groundbreaking research reveals how to embrace the hidden strength of positive emotions, overcome negativity, and thrive.* New York: Crown.

Gallup. (2017). Gallup student poll: Engaged today—ready for tomorrow, U.S. over-all. Retrieved from https://www.gallup.com/file/education/233681/2017 GSP Scorecard.pdf

Gaser, C., & Schlaug, G. (2003, October 8). Brain structures differ between musicians and non-musicians. *Journal of Neuroscience, 23*(27), 9240–9245. doi:10.1523/JNEUROSCI.23-27-09240.2003

Germuth, A. A. (2012). *Helping all learners reach their potential: What teachers say about graduate programs that integrate the implications of mind, brain, and education research.* Orlando, FL: BrainSMART.

Goleman, D. (2015). *Focus: The hidden driver of excellence.* New York: HarperCollins.

Good, C., Aronson, J., & Inzlicht, M. (2003). Improving adolescents' standard-ized test performance: An intervention to reduce the effects of stereotype threat. *Applied Developmental Psychology, 24*(6), 645–662.

Grant, H., & Dweck, C. S. (2003). Clarifying achievement goals and their impact. *Journal of Personality and Social Psychology, 85*(3), 541–553.

Guskey, T. R. (2002). Professional development and teacher change. *Teachers and Teaching, 8*(3), 381–391. doi:10.1080/135406002100000512

Halvorson, H. G. (2012). *Succeed: How we can reach our goals.* New York: Plume.

Harvard Graduate School of Education. (2015). *Growth mindset and grit liter-ature review.* Wellington Learning and Research Centre. Retrieved from https://belmontteach.files.wordpress.com/2015/09/growth-mindset-and-grit-lit-review.pdf

Hattie, J. (2012). *Visible learning for teachers: Maximizing impact on learning.* New York: Routledge.

Hattie, J., & Anderman, E.M. (2020). *Visible learning: Guide to student achieve-ment.* New York: Routledge.

Hattie, J., & Timperley, H. (2007). The power of feedback. *Review of Educational Research, 77*(1), 81–112. doi: 10.3102/003465430298487

Hecht, D. (2013, September). The neural basis of optimism and pessimism. *Experimental Neurobiology, 22*(3), 173–199.

Hendrickx, M. M., Mainhard, M. T., Boor-Klip, H. J., Cillessen, A. H., & Brekelmans, M. (2016). Social dynamics in the classroom: Teacher support and conflict and the peer ecology. *Teaching and Teacher Education, 53,* 30–40. doi:10.1016/j.tate.2015.10.004

Hennessey, J. (2016). *Motivation beyond the lab: The effect of motivation interven-tions in school settings.* Mindset Scholars Network. Retrieved from http://mindsetscholarsnetwork.org/wp-content/uploads/2016/05/Motivation_Beyond_The_Lab_Brief.pdf

Immordino-Yang, M. H. (2016). *Emotions, learning, and the brain: Exploring the educational implications of affective neuroscience.* New York: Norton.

Immordino-Yang, M. H., & Damasio, A. R. (2016). We feel, therefore we learn: The relevance of affect and social neuroscience to education. In M. H. Immordino-Yang (Ed.), *Emotions, learning, and the brain: Exploring the educational implications of affective neuroscience* (pp. 27–42). New York: Norton.

Immordino-Yang, M. H., Darling-Hammond, L., & Krone, C. (2018). *The brain basis for integrated social, emotional, and academic development: How emotions and social relationships drive learning.* Aspen, CO: The Aspen Institute. Retrieved from https://assets.aspeninstitute.org/content/uploads/2018/09/Aspen_research_FINAL_web-9.20.pdf

Immordino-Yang, M. H., & Faeth, M. (2010). The role of emotion and skilled intuition in learning. In D. A. Sousa (Ed.), *Mind, brain, and education* (pp. 69–84). Bloomington, IN: Solution Tree.

International Association for Cognitive Education and Psychology. (2016). What is cognitive education? Retrieved from http://ia-cep.org/about-us/about-us-iacep

Koch, R. (2014). *The 80/20 principle and 92 other powerful laws of nature.* Boston: Nicholas Brealey Publishing.

Lahey, Jessica. (2016, May 4). To help students learn, engage the emotions. *New York Times.* Retrieved from https://well.blogs.nytimes.com/2016/05/04/to-help-students-learn-engage-the-emotions/

Latham, G. (n.d.). *The value of goal setting for students.* The Pacific Institute. Retrieved from http://educationinitiative.thepacificinstitute.com/articles/story/the-value-of-goal-setting-for-students

Lazowski, R. A., & Hulleman, C. S. (2016, June 1). Motivation interventions in education: A meta-analytic review. *Review of Educational Research, 86*(2), 602–640. doi: 10.3102/0034654315617832

Long, H. (2016, April 12). The new normal: 4 job changes by the time you're 32. *CNN Business.* Retrieved from https://money.cnn.com/2016/04/12/news/economy/millennials-change-jobs-frequently/index.html

Maule, L. (2009). The art and science of designing engaging work. *PAGE One, 31*, 24–26.

Merzenich, M. (2013). *Soft-wired: How the new science of brain plasticity can change your life* (2nd ed.). San Francisco: Parnassus.

Morisano, D., Hirsh, J. B., Peterson, J. B., Pihl, R. O., & Shore, B. M. (2010). Setting, elaborating, and reflecting on personal goals improves academic performance. *Journal of Applied Psychology, 95*(2), 255–264.

Mueller, C. M., & Dweck C. S. (1998). Praise for intelligence can undermine children's motivation and performance. *Journal of Personality and Social Psychology, 75*(1), 33–52.

National Academies of Sciences, Engineering, and Medicine. (2018). *How people learn II: Learners, contexts, and cultures.* Washington, DC: The National Academies Press. doi: 10.17226/24783

National Association of Independent Schools. (Winter 2008). *You can grow your intelligence.* Retrieved from https://www.nais.org/magazine/independent-school/winter-2008/you-can-grow-your-intelligence

National Research Council & Institute of Medicine. (2004). *Engaging schools: Fostering high school students' motivation to learn.* Washington, DC: The National Academies Press. Retrieved from www.nap.edu/books/0309084350/html

O'Keefe, P. A., Dweck, C. S., & Walton, G. M. (2018a, September 10). Having a growth mindset makes it easier to develop new interests. *Harvard Business Review.* Retrieved from https://hbr.org/2018/09/having-a-growth-mindset-makes-it-easier-to-develop-new-interests

O'Keefe, P. A., Dweck, C. S., & Walton, G. M. (2018b, October 1). Implicit theories of interest: Finding your passion or developing it? *Psychological Science, 29*(10), 1653–1664. doi:10.1177/0956797618780643

Organisation for Econonic Co-operation and Development. (2019). Programme for International Student Assessment (PISA): Results from PISA 2018 (Volumes 1–III), Country note: United States. Retrieved from http://www.oecd.org/pisa/publications/PISA2018_CN_USA.pdf

PERTS. (n.d.). *Growth mindset for 9th graders: A free, evidence-based program to increase students' engagement, motivation, and success by promoting a growth mindset.* Retrieved from https://neptune. perts.net/static/programs/hg17/information_packet.pdf

Piaget, J., & Inhelder, B. (1972). *The psychology of the child.* New York: Basic.

Positive Psychology Center. (2019). Welcome. Retrieved from https://ppc.sas.upenn.edu/

PositivePsychology.com. (2019, June 5). The 5 founding fathers and a history of positive psychology. Retrieved from https://positivepsychologyprogram.com/founding-fathers

Ratey, J. J., & Manning, R. (2015). *Go wild: Eat fat, run free, be social, and follow evolution's other rules for total health and well-being.* New York: Little, Brown Spark.

Riddle, D. R., & Lichtenwalner, R. J. (2007). Neurogenesis in the adult and aging brain. In D. R. Riddle (Ed.), *Brain aging: Models, methods and mechanisms* (Chapter 6). Boca Raton, FL: CRC. Retrieved from http://www.ncbi.nlm.nih.gov/books/NBK3874

Romero, C., Master, A., Paunesku, D., Dweck, C. S., & Gross, J. J. (2014). Academic and emotional functioning in middle school: The role of implicit theories. *Emotion, 14*(2), 227–234.

Scheffler, I. (2010). *Of human potential: An essay in the philosophy of education.* New York: Routledge.

Seligman, M. E. P. (1995). *The optimistic child: A proven program to safeguard children against depression and build lifelong resilience.* New York: Harper Perennial.

Seligman, M. E. P. (2006). *Learned optimism: How to change your mind and your life.* New York: Simon & Schuster.

Seligman, M. E. P. (2011). *Flourish: A visionary new understanding of happiness and well-being.* New York: Free Press.

Siegel, D. (2016). Dr. Daniel Siegel presenting a hand model of the brain [YouTube video]. Retrieved from https://www.youtube.com/watch?v=gm9CIJ74Oxw

Sternberg, R. J. (1999). The theory of successful intelligence. *Review of General Psychology, 3,* 292–316. doi:10.1037/1089-2680.3.4.292

Sternberg, R. J. (2018). The triarchic theory of successful intelligence. In D. P. Flanagan & E. M. McDonough (Eds.), *Contemporary intellectual assessment: Theories, tests, and issues* (p. 174–194). New York: Guilford Press.

Sternberg, R. J., Jarvin, L., & Grigorenko, E. L. (2015). *Teaching for wisdom, intelligence, creativity, and success.* New York: Skyhorse Publishing.

Sternberg, R. J., & Williams, W. M. (2010). *Educational psychology* (2nd ed.). Upper Saddle River, NJ: Pearson.

Svinicki, M. D. (2016). Motivation: An updated analysis. Retrieved from https://files.eric.ed.gov/fulltext/ED573640.pdf

Tokuhama-Espinosa, T. (2017, April 4). International Delphi panel survey on mind, brain, and education science. Quito, Ecuador: Author. Retrieved from https://drive.google.com/file/d/0B8RaPiQPEZ9ZVTZQbmxaNENJNHc/view

Tokuma-Espinosa, T. (2018). *Neuromyths: Debunking false ideas about the brain.* New York: Norton.

van Geert, P., & Steenbeck, H. (2008). Brains and the dynamics of "wants" and "cans" in learning. *Mind, Brain, and Education, 2*(2), 62–66.

Weiner, B. (1992). *Human motivation: Metaphors, theories, and research* (Revised ed.). Thousand Oaks, CA: Sage.

Weiner, B. (2018). The legacy of an attribution approach to motivation and emotion: A no-crisis zone. *Motivation Science, 4*(1), 4–14. doi.org/10.1037/mot0000082

Weir, K. (2011, December). The exercise effect. *American Psychological Association Monitor, 42*(11). Retrieved from https://www.apa.org/monitor/2011/12/exercise

Wiggins, G. (2012, September). Seven keys to effective feedback. *Educational Leadership 70*(1), 10–16. Retrieved from: http://www.ascd.org/publications/educational-leadership/sept12/vol70/num01/Seven-Keys-to-Effective-Feedback.aspx

Willis, J., & Willis, M. (2020). *Research-based strategies to ignite student learning: Insights from neuroscience and the classroom* (2nd ed.). Alexandria, VA: ASCD.

Wilson, D. L. (2012). Training the mind's eye: "Brain movies" support comprehension and recall. *The Reading Teacher, 66.* doi:10.1002/TRTR.01091

Wilson, D. L. (2017, May 12). Keynote Jamaica, Dr. Donna Wilson. [YouTube video]. Retrieved from https://www.youtube.com/watch?v=Igg_j7re7qE

Wilson, D. L., & Conyers, M. A. (2013a). *Effective teaching, successful students: Graduates share how earning their M.S. and Ed.S. degrees with majors in brain-based teaching guides their professional practice.* Orlando, FL: BrainSMART.

Wilson, D. L., & Conyers, M. A. (2013b). *Effective teaching, successful students: Graduates share how earning their M.S. and Ed.S. degrees with majors in brain-based teaching guides their professional practice* [Kindle version]. Orlando, FL: BrainSMART.

Wilson, D. L., & Conyers, M. A. (2014a, October). The boss of my brain. *ASCD Educational Leadership 72*(2). Retrieved from http://www.ascd.org/

publications/educational-leadership/oct14/vol72/num02/£The-Boss-of-My- Brain£.aspx

Wilson, D. L., & Conyers, M. A. (2014b, March 12). Move your body, grow your brain. Edutopia. Retrieved from https://www.edutopia.org/blog/move-body-grow-brain-donna-wilson

Wilson, D. L., & Conyers, M. A. (2015, February 12). Putting working memory to work in learning. Edutopia. Retrieved from https://www.edutopia.org/blog/put-working-memory-to-work-donna-wilson-marcus-conyers

Wilson, D. L., & Conyers, M. A. (2016a). *Teaching students to drive their brains: Metacognitive strategies, activities, and lesson ideas*. Alexandria, VA: ASCD.

Wilson, D. L., & Conyers, M. A. (2016b, November 8). The teenage brain is wired to learn—so make sure your students know it. Edutopia. Retrieved from https://www.edutopia.org/article/teenage-brain-is-wired-to-learn-donna-wilson-marcus-conyers

Wilson, D. L., & Conyers, M. A. (2016c, December 2). Simple ways to help young kids develop self-control. Edutopia. Retrieved from https://www.edutopia.org/article/simple-ways-to-help-young-kids-develop-self-control-donna-wilson-marcus-conyers

Wilson, D. L., & Conyers, M. A. (2018). *BrainSMART 60 strategies for boosting test scores* (5th ed.). Moorabbin, Victoria, Australia: Hawker Browlow.

Wilson, D. L., & Conyers, M. A. (2020). *Five big ideas for effective teaching: Connecting mind, brain, and education research to classroom practice* (2nd ed.). New York: Teachers College Press.

Woollett, K., & Maguire, E. A. (2011). Acquiring "the knowledge" of London's layout drives structural brain changes. *Current Biology, 21*(24), 2109–2114. doi:10.1016/j.cub.2011.11.018

World Economic Forum. (2018). *The future of jobs report: 2018*. Key findings. Centre for the New Economy and Society. Geneva, Switzerland: Author. Retrieved from http://reports.weforum.org/future-of-jobs-2018/key-findings/?doing_wp_cron=1559133711.97469496726989 74609375

Yeager, D. S., & Dweck, C. S. (2012). Mindsets that promote resilience: When students believe that personal characteristics can be developed. *Educational Psychologist, 47*(4), 302–314. doi:10.1080/00461520.2012.722805

Zimmer, C. (2014, August 19). Doublethink: The slight differences between the hemispheres may soup up the brain's processing power. *Discover*. Retrieved from https://www.discovermagazine.com/the-sciences/doublethink

Index

Note: The letter *f* following a page number denotes a figure.

About the Authors

Donna Wilson, PhD, psychologist and author, is an international speaker on developing growth mindsets, supporting social-emotional learning, and teaching practical strategies that are essential for surviving and thriving in the world today. Growing up in rural Oklahoma, Donna was the first in her family to go to college; she went on to become the Chair of Education at the University of Detroit-Mercy and later cofounded and became president of BrainSMART®, Inc. and the nonprofit Center for Innovative Education and Prevention. With her passion for empowering all learners with the science and strategies for achieving academic and life success, Donna co-developed the world's first graduate degree programs in applied mind, brain, and education science (BrainSMART Programs) and doctoral minor in brain-based leadership. Over the past 20 years, she has shared her work with more than 60,000 participants in live events in Asia, the Middle East, Australia, Europe, Jamaica, and throughout the United States and Canada. She serves on the foundation of Carl Albert State College in Oklahoma and on the Advisory Board for Portfolio School in New York City. Donna is the author of 20 books, including *Teaching Students*

to Drive Their Brains (ASCD, 2016), *Five Big Ideas for Effective Teaching* (Teachers College Press, 2nd edition in press), *Positively Smarter* (Wiley, 2015), and *Introduction to BrainSMART Teaching* (Hawker Browlow Education, 2017). You can contact Donna at donna@brainsmart.org, view her blog at http://donnawilsonphd. blogspot.com/, or connect with her on LinkedIn (Donna Wilson, PhD), and Facebook (Donna Wilson Conyers).

Marcus Conyers, PhD, is a research supervisor for the PhD in Professional Practice: Psychological Perspectives at the Salomons Institute for Applied Psychology with Canterbury Christ Church University and the lead developer of the BrainSMART® and Innovating Minds® programs for improving cognitive performance and creative-thinking skills. Marcus earned his doctorate with a focus on innovative applications of mind, brain, and education science from the University of Westminster. He is the lead developer of the world's first doctoral minor in brain-based leadership and the first MS and EdS degree programs focused on applied mind, brain, and education science (BrainSMART Programs). Central to Marcus's work is the belief that developing growth mindsets is key to increasing the creative and critical thinking skills that drive higher levels of human performance. Founder and CEO of BrainSMART and the nonprofit Center for Innovative Education and Prevention, Conyers is an author of 20 books who has worked in 30 countries and shared his innovative frameworks with more than 100,000 people on five continents. In addition to the ministers of education in South Africa, the United Arab Emirates, and Ontario, Canada, his audiences have included Navy Seals, Army Rangers, counterintelligence operatives, law enforcement officers, and business leaders globally. His passion is improving lives through innovative applications of the cognitive and implementation sciences, and he serves as the director of the nonprofit Center for Innovative Education and Prevention. You can contact Marcus

at marcus@brainsmart.org. You can visit his website—http://
www.innovatingminds.org/—where you will also find his blog, and
you can connect with him on LinkedIn.

You can find Donna Wilson and Marcus Conyers on the web at
www.brainsmart.org, on Facebook at BrainSMART, and you can
follow them on Twitter @BrainSMARTU and on Pinterest at
BrainSMARTU.

Related ASCD Resources

At the time of publication, the following resources were available (ASCD stock numbers appear in parentheses):

Print Products

Teaching Students to Drive Their Brains: Metacognitive Strategies, Activities, and Lesson Ideas by Donna Wilson and Marcus Conyers (#117002)

Engage the Brain: How to Design for Learning That Taps into the Power of Emotion by Allison Posey (#119015)

Upgrade Your Teaching: Understanding by Design Meets Neuroscience by Jay McTighe and Judy Willis (119008)

Differentiation and the Brain: How Neuroscience Supports the Learner-Friendly Classroom, 2nd Edition, by David A. Sousa and Carol Ann Tomlinson (#318125)

Teaching with the Brain in Mind, 2nd Edition, by Eric Jensen (#104013)

Teaching with Poverty in Mind: What Being Poor Does to Kids' Brains and What Schools Can Do About It by Eric Jensen (#109074)

For up-to-date information about ASCD resources, go to www.ascd.org. You can search the complete archives of *Educational Leadership* at www.ascd.org/el.

ASCD myTeachSource®

Download resources from a professional learning platform with hundreds of research-based best practices and tools for your classroom at http://myteachsource.ascd.org/.

For more information, send an e-mail to member@ascd.org; call 1-800-933-2723 or 703-578-9600; send a fax to 703-575-5400; or write to Information Services, ASCD, 1703 N. Beauregard St., Alexandria, VA 22311-1714 USA.

THE WHOLE CHILD

The ASCD Whole Child approach is an effort to transition from a focus on narrowly defined academic achievement to one that promotes the long-term development and success of all children. Through this approach, ASCD supports educators, families, community members, and policymakers as they move from a vision about educating the whole child to sustainable, collaborative actions.

Developing Growth Mindsets relates to the **engaged**, **supported**, and **challenged** tenets. *For more about the ASCD Whole Child approach, visit* **www.ascd.org/wholechild**.

WHOLE CHILD TENETS

1 HEALTHY
Each student enters school healthy and learns about and practices a healthy lifestyle.

2 SAFE
Each student learns in an environment that is physically and emotionally safe for students and adults.

3 ENGAGED
Each student is actively engaged in learning and is connected to the school and broader community.

4 SUPPORTED
Each student has access to personalized learning and is supported by qualified, caring adults.

5 CHALLENGED
Each student is challenged academically and prepared for success in college or further study and for employment and participation in a global environment.